VIEW FROM THIS WILDERNESS

Books by John Sanford:

The Water Wheel, 1933
The Old Man's Place, 1935
Seventy Times Seven, 1939
The People from Heaven, 1943
A Man Without Shoes, 1951
The Land That Touches Mine, 1953
Every Island Fled Away, 1964
The $300 Man, 1967
A More Goodly Country, 1975
Adirondack Stories, 1976
View From This Wilderness, 1977

View
From
This
Wilderness
American Literature as History

JOHN SANFORD

Neither could they go up to the top of Pisgah,
to view from this wilderness a more goodly
country to feed their hopes.
— WM. BRADFORD
HISTORY OF PLYMOUTH PLANTATION

foreword by PAUL MARIANI

CAPRA PRESS / *Santa Barbara*

Several of these pieces first appeared in *A More Goodly Country*, published in 1975. For permission to reprint them here, grateful acknowledgment is made to Mr. Ben Raeburn of Horizon Press.

Library of Congress Cataloging in Publication Data

Sanford, John B   1904-
 View from this wilderness.

 1. United States—History—Literary collections. 2. American literature—History and criticism—Addresses, essays, lectures. 3. Authors, American—Literary collections. I. Title.
PS3537.A694V5   810'8   77-23835
ISBN 0-88496-112-5

CAPRA PRESS
631 State Street
Santa Barbara, CA 93101

Joseph Moncure March   1899-1977

Dalton Trumbo   1905-1976

Edwin Rolfe   1909-1954

Henry Bamford Parkes   1904-1972

IN THEIR MEMORY

CONTENTS

FOREWORD

Rather the ice than their way.

Thus William Carlos Williams some half century ago, fleshing Eric the Red, the old world outcast in the new, at the start of *In the American Grain.* This self-reflective gesture spoke deeply then to Williams' need to tell it his way rather than theirs—"theirs" being the academy, the wide-circulation journals—to provide instead his own key for unlocking the treasures and ghoul chests which constitute our American past. And so too with Sanford's splendid trilogy,* his prose poem epic evoking that compound, familiar and forgotten ghost we call our heritage.

The alignment with Williams is intentional, since Sanford has dedicated the first volume of that trilogy—*A More Goodly Country*—to the memory of Williams, and has generously provided us with a sense of just how deep his debt goes when he tells us in this middle volume, *View from This Wilderness,* that in fifty years he has been able to read *In the American Grain* only once, so profoundly did that book affect him. But though encountered once in that sense, it has provided him with a way of organizing, of shaping the thousand thousand particulars, the thick stew, the flotsam and jetsam we call the data of history:

> And then into that random, that strew of phrases,
> tables, dates, and places—a conjunctive for scattered
> times and disparate faces, a strand for all those teeth
> and beads and shells of history, a book for books to be
> written by. . . . You remembered how it made still
> things stir for you, how they'd seemed to sort
> themselves, how they'd begun to fall in line. . . .

But if Williams is there as progenitor, this son has learned his lesson well, and—in part by the very nature of his meditation, in part by the sheer duration of that meditation—has managed to achieve in his trilogy a distinctive, idiosyncratic, iconoclas-

---

A More Goodly Country (1975); the present volume, *View from This Wilderness* (1977); and *To Feed Their Hopes* (to be published in 1978).

13

tic, and lasting masterpiece of American literature. What Sanford has done in all three books—for the underlying strategy throughout is a shimmering constant—is to take thousands of scraps from our literary past—the sodden pages of brown-edged second rate novels, travel journals, court decisions, the tall bawdy tales of the frontier, those texts we call our classics, sermons, diaries, letters, saccharine missives, fragments of poems, biographies, autobiographies, dime novels, histories, pamphlets, tracts, newspapers, essays, old photos— has taken these rummaged scraps from the grab-bag of history and blown a new and exciting life into them. Each becomes, then, an independent frame in this cinematic epic, ranging in length from several pages to a marvellously wrought tone poem in a single paragraph.

What distinguishes these three volumes, finally, is Sanford's emphasis in each. *A More Goodly Country*, published in 1975, has the subtitle, *A Personal History of America*, and begins, as Williams does, with Eric being hounded from Iceland. It moves through a millenium to that moment in mid-1945 when Truman gave the signal to create nuclear Armageddon over Hiroshima and Nagasaki, an outcome we might have read in the seeds of our beginnings. In this unfolding of our history, Sanford sketches deftly the famous and infamous and forgotten, our explorers and statesmen, religious and military leaders, victors and victims, artists and artisans, the man on the street and underdogs of every description. Here, jostling each other, the most unlikely characters strut or limp side by side: Columbus and Coronado; the dwarf anti-slavery Quaker, Lay, and Hawthorne's Pearl; Eugene Debs and Tom Mooney; Tom Paine and Chivington of the Sand Creek Massacre; Boss Tweed and Josiah Willard Gibbs; Isadora Duncan and the Molly Maguires; Teddy Roosevelt and Pancho Villa; Charlie Chaplin and Woodrow Wilson—all amidst the verbal splendor of Sanford's lifetime spent gleaning our past.

The present volume, *View from This Wilderness*, reads the wealth of American Literature—widely understood—as history, and it will be the primary task of this Foreword to speak of Sanford's achievement in effecting that reading. But a word first about the third book of the Sanford trilogy, *To Feed Their Hopes,* which may well prove to be the most readily acceptable of the three, at least in the immediate future, for that book deals with the history of American women. All kinds of women, from the near mythic and famous, to the unknown and those known personally to Sanford himself. A great cross-section of women, fictive presences, wives, mothers, financiers, working girls, novelists, poets, dancers, charlatans, Indians, the wives of Indian killers, Indian captives, and the countless victims—for America has not dealt kindly with its women. But what is most amazing about this panorama of women—drawn from novels, photos, histories, even from memory—is that no two portraits are alike, so well has this writer avoided the stereotype, the typical cameo.

Sanford is a generous writer and has given us more than one hundred and twenty portraits, separate voices, in *View from This Wilderness,* spanning the whole creation of America, from the first words of Columbus after he had actually found the new world he was seeking, to the death of John Berryman in January 1972, when his body crashed against the steep rocks on its way down to the frozen Mississippi, that river which holds so much of our history. Only someone who had meditated long and hard on the significance of place as shaper would have bestowed the meticulous care evident in Sanford's culling all of those out-of-the-way sources, in spending so many years manipulating such a gorgeous array of clickering, antiphonal voices, and as Williams before him had, in allowing so many of these figures to speak for themselves. Again, only a catalog can begin to demonstrate the range of presences which Sanford has blooded in this book. There are the known: from characters like Mather, Hawthorne, Edward Taylor, the Adamses—Sam and Henry, to Jefferson, Poe and Thoreau, to Whitman, Henry James, Teddy Roosevelt and the Cranes—Stephen and Hart; from Jack London and Dreiser and Frost and Stein, to Sandburg, Stevens, Pound and Eliot. And there are, too, the unknown or lesser known: from figures like Prescott, Harriot, Winthrop, Père Le Jeune, Otis, Parkman, and Timrod, to Tourgée, Helper, Woolson, Lazarus, Brann, Brisbane,

15

Ehrlich. But each section, each frame, manages to open up a different world, which, though complete within itself, also illuminates and passes judgment on those worlds to either side.

* * *

Reading Sanford's trilogy, I am reminded of an image evoked by Sartre in meditating on Faulkner's sense of history: that the eye tends there to perceive all history as if from the back of a speeding train, where the attention is drawn towards remarking an ever-receding past, so that even the most approximate present can be seen only as it clarifies itself by moving backwards, towards the horizon, to a point already past. When I apply this sense of the past to Sanford, however, I am only partially satisfied. In my reading, Sanford seems preoccupied if not obsessed with the sense of telos, the sense of something already completed, cut off, ripe for being weighed in the scales of history. (It is just here, incidentally, that he seems to differ so radically from someone like Williams, whose dictum to begin again suggests instead generativity, the gesture of initiation.) Sanford's characteristic gesture of resurrecting the dead often carries with it the sense of the author blowing a kind of momentary flickering life into these bones, this dried-out rotting skull with its mat of curling hair.

Consider this: though published in 1975, *A More Goodly Country* refuses to inch any closer to our present than 1945. The reason, I think, is that '45 is the watershed date, both for Sanford as a man and for us as a nation. For that is the year in which Sanford remembers, in the loss of 6,000,000 exterminated Jews, his own dead mother (a year, then, in which his own sense of his past must have been called into agonizing reappraisal); the year when one very real apocalypse arrived, when President Roosevelt having died, his replacement ordered the new American super power to demonstrate its supremacy by dropping a new kind of bomb on Japan; the year, too, when we brought one of our greatest American poets home from his exile for trial after first de-humanizing him by keeping him in a gorilla cage in Pisa. But Sanford himself suggests why he has chosen 1945 in his invocation of Charlie Chaplin, for if

16

half a millenium of our history has taught us anything, it is that the future will continue to hold "more of the same, the last stuffed club, the last splash of mud, the last stumble, the saunter toward the final fall." The Hart Crane who composed "Chaplinesque" would have understood.

And so too with *View from This Wilderness,* which is also markedly retrospective, not only in terms of its pastness, but in terms of that preoccupation of Sanford's—and often of his characters—with their own ends, with the posture they hold as they pass from this life into death. If you would learn who and what we are, Sanford insists, then look to our past. Look to the records, he proclaims, with the percussive eloquence of an Ezekiel, a Jeremiah, an Isaiah, look to these shards, fragments, ciphers on musty, yellowing paper, look too to the strange, luminous phosphorescence emanating from these dead . . . and read yourselves. For in this handful of dust is contained the seeds that came in time to flower in us. We, then, are the promised issue, the future beyond themselves towards which they looked, though that future has probably not turned out as they had hoped. There is something particularly poignant, for example, in Columbus, as arch-original voice, reiterating plaintively in his journal that, look as long and as hard as he may, he can find "no gold, no gold," even as Sanford makes us see all around us the "tall green trees/ that bathe the tired eye," and "Parrots [that] in their numbers/ would have dimmed the sky/ had not their colors blazed it," and shows us all manner of wonders (it is, ironically, Columbus himself recording these things): "a creature like unto a pig,/ all shell and very hard,/ soft only at the neck and eyes" (a sea turtle?), and purslane, wild amaranth, dogs that never bark.

Sanford of course knows there is gold here, has counted the costs along his own pulse, in his long hours of attention to his craft and to those mountains of documents, so that he continues to evoke our new world promise, to point to all that gold there before us which we, in our peculiar blindness, seldom ever see. But this man knows what he is after, and—hawk's eye that he has—can gather from the vacant spaces of our past those honest, quiet presences which haunt him—and now us—as in his

17

meditation on the good Indian preacher, John Eliot. If, digging into the dust of that distant past, all that remains is the "nail and hair of a parish preacher, his entrail dust and phalangeal bone," Sanford lovingly pieces the man together among the dance of his own syllables, as in this passage (which may be more autobiographical than Sanford intended):

> It'd been love's labor, his three-score years in the Roxbury pulpit, his journeys to the Praying Towns, his winters among the wigwams in the pines; love's labor, his learning to speak a language that was spoken only, that was gone with the going of its sound; love's labor, a gift of the heart. . . .

A new birth in this new world, then, together with a new language which might have wed with the one already here. A marrying with those already here: the great possibility for Sanford as it had been too for Williams, as in his portraits of Père Sebastian Rasles and Daniel Boone. But a gesture all-in-all refused. Refused by Captain John Smith, so that Pokahontas, though married to another, fell away because of Smith's gesture of refusal. Refused too by Increase Mather, who talked away as many life-supporting systems as his long years allowed, including all sorts of innocent rituals and those departures from a strict regimen of work, managing finally, even to talk Christmas itself away, and who, had he been given time, "might 've outproved Hospinian: he might've shown that no Savior had arrived at all." But that refusal runs deep, finds its echo down the centuries, not only in Hawthorne's Reverend Dimmesdale and many of the puritan elders, where we might expect it (so that it is no wonder that there are accounts of bestiality and consorting with the "savage"), but also in figures as diverse as John Marshall, refusing to hear the legality of a case against the young Republic that the revolution had done away with special interest groups and monopolies, that this land belonged to the people (a joke, such a notion). Or those others, like Francis Parkman, Teddy Roosevelt and Ernest Hemingway, who all held that you had to kill a thing—a crane, a wren, a buffalo, an Indian—before it was safe enough to be observed as

18

a thing of beauty. Or, finally, figures like Timrod, Hinton Rowan Helper, and Jack London, all of whom in their own way let it be known that the Black man had to be kept in his rightful place. With the Indian gone, we find ourselves in Manila, Tokyo, Saigon. With the buffalo decimated, Teddy will find himself in Africa, like Hemingway after him:

> On the Kapiti plain, the Kikuyus heard a great crashing all through that year, and it was heard too in the Rift, and among the Nyanza reeds, and in Jubaland it was heard beside the running streams—yea, a great crashing came from the yews and aloes and euphorbias, for game was falling in all those places, oryxes, klipspringers, elands, rhinos, giraffes, oribis, gazelles, the last of these graced with lyrelike horns, an embrace, they seemed to be.

One corollary to this great refusal is that we find ourselves more than half in love with death, strenuous in the case of the enemy, easeful in our own, as if we had already surrendered, had given over our will to live. This dismal fact may help explain why so many of Sanford's figures are evoked either near or at the moment of death. Or, barring this, they yearn towards that time, their own moment having flickered past, the years remaining a sad waste time after. Beyond these manifestations is the recurrent gesture of the author digging up their dusty graves or breaking into their tombs to search for some clue, some secret center to sum up a lifetime's action. And it is just here that this fervent, angry archaeologist who will not let the past settle into some dusty oblivion, it is just here that I am most reminded of Dante. For, if we take anything beyond our Sunday-best suit of soon-mildewed cloth and our parchment-yellow skin with us into that grave, it is our moral acts—though done without fanfare or in secret—which determine our lasting worth for good or otherwise. "What, are you here?" Dante addresses Ser Brunetto Latini, his old teacher, in hell for assorted acts of buggery despite his great service to humanism. And so with Sanford. Life is a shadow and it swiftly goes, throwing up images on some diorama, silver screen or Plato's cave. But that act—that inscaping, essential, telling moral act—abides under this scrutinist's eye.

This insistence on judgment, of course, leads to a kind of heaven and a kind of hell, with a purgatory of sorts and even a limbo for that multitude incapable of making a choice either way. There are bound to be some surprises in the construction of any such afterlife; this is as true for Blake as it is for Dante or Pound or Williams... or Sanford. Sanford's deepest sympathies are unquestionably with the people, the people as Sandburg or Lincoln or Reed or Christ would have understood the term, the downtrodden democratic masses. And Sanford's sympathies lying just here, we should not be surprised to find that his own pantheon, his own community of saints, should include such diverse figures as John Eliot, Apostle to the Indians, Katherine Tekakwitha,* Edward Taylor (invoked with an oblique salute to Hopkins) and that half-literate defender of a free press, John Peter Zenger, Albion Tourgée and the nun of Amherst, Emma Lazarus and Bessie Smith,* John Reed and Randolph Bourne, Sacco and Vanzetti: all those who acted as smaller-case christs in their ministerings, sufferings, and witness. If one has the eyes to see. Consider this one example, the doctor who ministered to Emily Dickinson in her last sickness:

> It was a high wide world, the room she lay in, and the
> sights it held he never descried. There were wilds
> inside the wall, there were rare shores and private
> ports of call, and he strode unaware among flowers,
> flights of bees, birds achant in a virgin mode. In that
> world of hers, he breathed love, not air, but what he
> sought there was Bowman's capsule, and what he
> found was a name for death—*Bright's disease.*

But Sanford's damned seem to outnumber his saints. These are the ones who yearned in their very marrow for death, for stasis, as they yeasted on the sour self. Among them, not only many of our puritan "saints," measured now by other standards, but Poe as well, and Thoreau, Timrod, Ambrose Bierce, Mary Baker Eddy, Lincoln Steffens, Faulkner, Hemingway,

---

*From *To Feed Their Hopes.*

Lionel Trilling, John O'Hara. Consider the case of Ambrose Bierce. It was *only* death he sought, Sanford tells us, that "bright and brass-buttoned Angel. He failed to find it at Corinth and Shiloh, failed again at Stone River, failed once more at Kenesaw, though there, with a Minié-ball in his head, it came close to finding him." He found it, finally, what he'd longed for all his life, there on the Rio Grande, the Styx, the Black Water . . . or it found him.

The other side of the penny we keep to hold the eyelids shut and to pay for Charon's fare across the river, is, perhaps, the elegiac tribute. I know of few who can sing those who have departed over the wide waters as movingly as Sanford, whether it be a kaddish for his young mother gone over these sixty years—*bes yisroel baagolo uvisman koriv v'imru Omen*—or remembering back to his highschool days at De Witt Clinton and those two Blacks, the only two Blacks in a world of white, one with a pistol hidden in his coat, and the other one who tried "to sing, to soar on lyrics till the pull of *g* was nil," Countee Cullen, gone himself these thirty years. Or these lines for Bessie Smith, blues for a blues singer: "In a hundred and sixty blues, black and bottomless sloughs of grief, her slurred elegies quaver, her lament for strayed lover and love betrayed, for hard times and harder coming—struck copper, that voice of hers, and listening, you forget to swallow. . . ." One of the most touching of the elegies in these elegiac books, however, is the one tinged with personal memory, a quiet salute to the ghost of his old friend, Pep West, Miss Lonelyhearts, remembered from '31, when he and West wrote their heads off in adjoining summer-shack rooms there on Viele Pond in the Adirondacks, "six miles west of Warrensburg on the way to Stony Creek":*

> Of that summer, buried under forty-five years, the only hard tokens are a spread of snapshots foxed now with age. In them, two figures stand, sit, lounge, two

---

*It was there, in that long-gone world, that Sanford wrote most of his *Adirondack Stories*, which William Carlos Williams, then editing *Contact* with the West, considered some of the best new writing to be found anywhere.   —P.M.

21

faces are fixed (on what? on whom?), hands hold sticks, a magazine, cigarettes, and an old car can be seen, and a porch, a doorway, a basin near a bench, and there are brown trees, sepia grass, and a tan sky. You have only to wait, you fancy, and you'll hear sound and witness motion. . . . But it won't do! it won't do! There'd be no change, though you looked and listened forever.

But Sanford *has* mediated brilliantly with that sense of stasis, this new world Prospero with his magic wand, has managed to nudge those long frozen scenes once more into shimmering movement. Again and again he achieves via his incandescent phrases, his marvellous word hoard, the same miracle for which he salutes Carl Sandburg, who managed in his biography of Lincoln what no subsequent biographer of Lincoln has been quite able to bring off: to raise this lower-case christ again from the dead. By the time Sandburg was finished with his myth, Sanford writes, there *was* a second Son, a second Christ. True, Lincoln's body lies there still in its Springfield earth, "slain and unrisen," dead "of a leaden bullet instead of iron nails." But for all that, in Sandburg's world, the man who "could make a cat laugh" lives again.

And so too with John Sanford, whose combined words in these three volumes act like seed cast on good ground. Not a verbal onanism—the stylistic wordplay of the self-contained artist locked into the self—but the onomastic gesture, the naming of the multitude of actors in our diverse, sprawling history, fleshing it out so that it lives again in these pages, just as Sanford's recovered, reactivated moral gestures from our past live. That these moral gestures may have been misunderstood, despised, rejected no longer matters; recovered and brought to the light once again for us, these acts shimmer with a new, resilient life. For despite Auden and the old New Critics and the various cliometricians, literature *can* make things happen—for better or worse.

View from This Wilderness, like its predecessor and its successor (for all three are cut from the same cloth, as their titles are all cut from the same passage of Bradford's *History of Plymouth Plantation)*, itself belongs to the Elect: with D. H. Lawrence's *Studies in Classic American Literature*, Williams' *In the American Grain*, and—in a narrower scope—with Berger's *Little Big Man*. Sanford deserves to be more widely known than he is, for he himself has made a kind of literary history with a trilogy as achieved and as ambitious as the writing of Dos Passos, MacLeish, and Robert Penn Warren when they worked in the American grain. Against the foregrounding roar of the big-circulation dailies this claim i .ay sound like a brave whistling in the dark, but that makes it no less true. It is one of the ironies of our own literary history (which is rife with such ironies), that it is only now, with Sanford in his seventies and still going strong, that the audience he deserves is beginning, at last, to shape itself. Since he himself learned long ago how to thrive, like his own cultural heroes, on failure, it is we Americans who have been the losers.

What we have been given, then, is his book, told in his way, with his own etched-out vision of this embittered, promised land. In half a century of relative isolation he has never swerved from Williams' dictum of the artist as exile in the new world: *Rather the ice than their way.*

Paul Mariani
University of Massachusetts
April 1977

Christopher Columbus, c.1446-1506

FIRST WORDS
IN THE NEW WORLD

being a continuation of the log
of the *Santa Maria*

*. . . And the others went running from house to house and to
the neighboring villages, with loud cries of 'Come, come to see
the people from Heaven!'*   —Christopher Columbus

Friday, 12th of October

I,
in order to delight them
and that I might preserve the concord
of our earliest intercourse,
gave to some of their number
certain articles of no great value,
which notwithstanding raptured them,
e.g.,
little red caps,
and beads of glass strung,
and cascabels of brass,
and these last they hung from the ear.
They are ardent for such trifles
and to obtain them from us
will offer all that they possess,
parrots,
spears, balls of bright-hued cotton,
aye, even their food itself.

Saturday, 13th of October

I labored to know if they knew of
gold.

Sunday, 14th of October

They are quite unskilled
in the use and care of arms,
and it misgives me not to say

25

that with scarcely fifty men,
I might keep them all in subjection.
The sea today was a tranquil round,
like the one to be found in a well.

Monday, 15th of October

Tales were told me of an island
whereon the people wore rings of gold,
and I set my sails for the place,
finding it fertile there, green,
and its breath was very soft,
and I bestowed brass timbrels
upon those who brought us water,
but no one knew what we meant by gold.

Tuesday, 16th of October

They bargain well, these people,
and they are seemly spoken,
tractable, industrious, trusting,
and having no creed of their own,
they could be speedily won
to Christianity.

Wednesday, 17th of October

What word I now get is of Samoet,
Samoet for gold, they say,
and for Samoet soon I sailed,
south by southwest, it lay,
and waiting to be found:
my find was the same as before,
more people but no gold.
A heavy rain fell.

Thursday, 18th of October

I weighed anchor at dawn
and laid a course to the southwest,
raising, before noon, another isle,
another Samoet,
the which I named *Isabella*,
and God grant it please her.

It is the loveliest thing ever seen,
with tall green trees
that bathe the tired eye,
and its perfumes tease our senses
from the shore.

Sunday, 21st of October

This day, at sun high, we went ashore,
and one would swear it Andalusia.
Parrots in their numbers
would have dimmed the sky
had not their colors blazed it,
and there were fruits, scented all,
and many other things of use,
such as medicinal herbs,
and I am the saddest man in the world
for knowing not their names.
We hear of a great isle called Colba.

Monday, 22nd of October

Some of the people wore pieces of gold,
or what resembled gold,
suspended from their nose,
and they bartered it for little things,
a broken cup,
a bit of earthenware,
a jingle for a sparrow-hawk,
but the amount of gold we got,
or what looked like gold,
was small.

Tuesday, 23rd of October

Colba being remindful of Cipango,
I was on fire to go there,
but the wind was wrong,
and I smoldered in the rain.

Wednesday, 24th of October

The rain gone and the wind right,
I made for Cipango

and the brisk trade in spices
I had heard of,
and the gold that abounded.
The wind bore us most lovingly.

Sunday, 28th of October
We raised the island, sailing near,
and then entering a lovely river
deep to either shore,
we anchored
seemingly within a forest.
The trees intermingled,
and we discerned flowers, fruit,
and small sweet-sung birds.
On going ashore, we joyed
in walking about in scent and song,
and we found purslane and wild amaranth
and dogs that never barked.
The people told us that ships came there
from the land of the Grand Khan,
doubtless, we thought, for pearls.

Friday, 2nd of November
I sent two men into the forest,
Rodrigo de Jerez, of Ayamonte,
and a certain Luis de Torres,
a converted Jew from Murcia
who understood Hebrew and Chaldee,
and they were given strings of beads
with which to purchase food,
and they were to seek out the King
and learn, if such fell their way,
the composition of his estate —
gold, pearls, spinels, &c.

Sunday, 4th of November
The two gone, people came to us
and spoke of a race in the forest
with one eye and the nose of a dog,

28

and these, they said, castrated a man
when they took him,
cut off his head,
and drank from both ends of him.

Tuesday, 6th of November
It pleased God this day
to return us Jerez and the Jew
with tales of things and the people
of the forest,
but they had nothing to say of gold.
There was no gold.

Friday, 16th of November
The men fished with nets
and took a creature like unto a pig,
all shell and very hard,
soft only at the neck and eyes,
but there was an opening underneath
for the voiding of superfluities.

Wednesday, 21st of November
No gold.

Sunday, 25th of November
No gold as yet. No gold. . . .

William Hickling Prescott, 1796-1859

QUETZALCOATL

A strange light broke forth in the east. It resembled a vast sheet or flood of fire. —William Hickling Prescott

The bright and burning tide was God returning from His journey to the sun. The blazon on the sea and sky was He, trailing golden rays and a tail of green-gold flame, and on the shore or wading in the waters, the people watched as the pageant came. Shepherd of the clouds, wind-guide, cause of thunder and cause of the cause, He was keeping his promise to Anahuac, He was coming back to earth!

> And by these signs were they to know Him
> When the daystar sent Him home from Tlapallan:
> He would wear a white gown, He said, a cloud
> Chosen from those in the blue wigwam overhead,
> And a flight of birds would bear Him company,
> And rare perfumes would mull the morning airs,
> And blooms would spring from dust, He said,
> And cotton flourish in vivid hues, and maize
> That men in pairs must portage like canoes —
> A gown from the wardrobe of the sky, He said,
> And spice on the wind, and flying minstrels...

To the people on the beach, all seemed to be as prophesied, even to the spice and the birds and the pungent songs they sang—it was paradise here! The meadows were green and deep, and they ran before the wind, flowed across the feet, and from vines among the trees, grapes in purple clusters hung, vignettes of coming wines, and honey-suckers (flower-kissers!) played in the flavored air, indeed the very air could be seen, so bright was it made by butterflies. It was paradise here! But the people, waiting for their dawn-God on the strand—*Hither-comes-whiteness-walking**—the people let the wrong god land.

---

*In one of the Amerind languages, the agglutination for *dawn*.

Thomas Harriot, 1560-1621

GOING HOME TO EDEN

To the Adventurers, Favorers, and Welwillers of the
Enterprise for the Inhabitting and Planting in Virginia:
                                        —Thomas Harriot

He knew the stars and, from the stars, the art of navigation, wherefore Grenville signed him on for the voyage, and he reached the shore of Virginia before Virginia Dare. A marvel of the day, the way he drew on the sun and the Great Bear for a route to Paradise, and a marvel still, how he found a channel that led through the bar. Five hundred ships have drowned off those banks, some in deep water and more in the surf, but he laid a course for land and damn near planned the passage in: it seemed to be waiting, and you'd've sworn he'd made it himself, pointed, by God, and put it there. . .!

  . . . *cedar, a sweet wood, is known in that place, meet for lute and good for virginale, and known as well two kinds of grape for two kinds of wine, and pitch and tarre abound, and walnutte oil and turpentine, and the soil doth yield the mordant alum, and there's woad for dyeing blue, and for dyeing red there's madder. Of peltries, a wealth is for the taking there, otters by the swimming shoal, and marternes, and beares, and deeres, of which the skins do dress like chamoes, soft as very love. And for suckets, there are savory gummes —the bdellium of Pison!—and let a man but dream on perles, and a stranded string lies in his hand. Rare herbes are common there, and terra sigillata, and silk on grass like the silk of Persia, and grains flourish, all sort and size, and mayze, and marigoldes, and a mort of mellions may be had, and there are tortoyses, crevises, and crabbes, and a weed, uppowoc, some call it, much used by Spaniardoes for the riddance of fleam, and there are rootes and fruit such as the medlar, and doves so numbrous fly as to black the high-noon skies. Go back, go you back to Paradise. . .!*

Though there was land beyond the land he lauded, vast, various, and many-shored, it was never known to him who'd so straightway found Virginia. The stars never shone him the heading, or the one they flashed he couldn't read—ah, well, he

31

was no seer, he was merely an astronomer. And yet, why could he not have seen ahead, read the hell in store for his Heaven? Why could he not tell of buffalo that would roam the range on nickels, small change to spend on trash, of Sioux who'd send up ciphers saying *Jesus Saves at 6%*? Why could he not tell of neon Eldorados of EAT DRINK BUY at the bottom of the sky, of heartbreak puled into microphones? Why could he not foresee the dead at every roadside, wrung and riven, blind, sprung, aghast at being offered up to the Okie of Things that Roll no More? Student at St. Mary's Hall, tutor to Raleigh's household, mathematician, navigator, star-gazer, caster of horoscopes, astrologaster, why could he not tell. . .?

Nathaniel Ward, 1578-1653

THE SIMPLE COBLER
OF AGGAWAM

How all Religions should enjoy their liberty in one Jurisdiction is beyond my comprehension.
—Nathaniel Ward

He was a cobler by trade, he said, and the claim made pages turn in the album of your mind. *Above a doorway, a gold boot swayed, and on a draft from the shop came the stench of glue, the nutgall tang of hides. On a bench inside, deep in skives, worn soles, broken laces, an old man was bent above a last that jutted up from his knees like a freak leg, a talipes. Aproned in leather, he seemed leathern too, and it might've been himself he sat tacking to a heel. Cornucopious, he was, with pegs issuing from his face as from the plenteous horn. . . .*
Aggawam is Ipswich now, and more than the name has gone, but some can show where his house once stood and his farm once groveled on stone, but they know not where he mended shoes. He was never a cobler, simple or otherwise. He was a parish parson out of Emmanuel, that crib of clerics, and he throve

32

there in England till he gagged on ritual, upthrew it, spewed it away, whereupon Laud stripped him of his rectory and with it his tithes and glebes. The Old World, alas, grew too hot for him, and, alack the day, Massachusetts proved too cold *(I am very deestitute,* he wrote to John Winthrop; *I have not aboue 6 bushells corne left.),* and want and the winds of winter sent the strayed shepherd home.

He was along in years by then, rising seventy, and a need for food and fire made him pen his screed. Laud was dead, headless in the grave, but death was the only difference now between the archbishop and his unfrocked pulpiteer. To the simple cobler, it didn't matter any more where the communion table was—let it be moved from place to place! let there be none at all!—nor did he care these days that churches dwelt in disrepair, or that antiphony, being music wed to prayer, had been bred beyond the Alps, spawned on the hills of Rome.

My heart, he avowed, *hath naturally detested Tolerations of divers Religions,* and his aversion came in Latin too—*Nullam malum pejus libertate errandi,* which is to say, the worst of freedoms is the freedom to err. Gone such figments as pincer and awl, and gone as well the scored and dingy ball of wax, and gone his crispin ruse, the back bowed over rundown shoes— gone the rebel, and in his stead the ruled. He kept his head, though, the cobler that never was, and unlike the patron saint, who stepped refreshed from boiling tar, he'd've boiled to a bubble, he'd've burst and died.

33

John Winthrop, 1588-1649

WINTHROP'S *JOURNAL*

being a selection from marginalia
found in a copy of the work

iv: A servant of one of our company had bargained with a child to sell him a box worth 3d. for three biscuits a day all the voyage, and had received about forty. . . .

What good to tie his hands to a bar on the deck of the *Arbella* and hang a basket of stones from his neck? what good to make him stand there, stooped over, whilst two hours passed? They got a look at the shape of his fud, but they saw nary a one of those forty biscuits.

ix: At the last court, a young fellow was whipped for soliciting an Indian squaw to incontinency. . . .

Was it worth what he paid for it, a dozen of the best and well laid on? did she bite him and buck, make him fight for his life, or did she lie like a wife, her thighs quite still? did she delight him with cries, did she clamp and claw him and upside-down her eyes? did she draw, when they kissed, a blister of blood, or did she come coldly while he hotly went?—oh, and was she built plumb with the world or level, like a Chink?

xii: At Watertown there was a great combat between a mouse and a snake; and, after a long fight, the mouse prevailed and killed the snake. Mr. Wilson, a very sincere, holy man, gave this interpretation: That the snake was the devil; the mouse was a poor contemptible people. . . .

Ah, it was there, then, that the Darkness Prince was shown the Light, there that Evil ended. Watertown, you say? W-a-t-e-r . . .?

xx: The scarcity of workmen had caused them to raise their wages. Many spent much time idly, because they could get as much in four days as would keep them a week. . . .

Solution: Double their hours or halve their pay, and if that doesn't do it, shoot them.

xxi: Robert Cole, having been oft punished for drunkenness, was now ordered to wear a red D about his neck for a year. . . .

Did the *D* in its rounds ever meet an *A*? That would've been a red-letter day.

xxv: A wicked fellow, given up to bestiality, fled to Long Island, and there was drowned. He had confessed to some, that he never saw any beast go before him but he lusted after it. . . .

Drowned, the poor bugger? Well, he was bound to come to a bad end.

lxi: One Hugh Bewett was banished for holding publicly that he was free from original sin and actual also. . . .

A second Christ and banished only! Where was the faith of old in the power of pain? He should've been rushed through all fourteen stations of another Passion!

35

lxv: A godly maid of the church of Linne, going in a deep snow from Meadford homeward, was lost, and some of her clothes found after among the rocks. . . .

To other godly maids of Linne, if you have to sinne, don't bare your asse—it gets ungodly cold in Meadford, Mass.

lxx: Mr. Hopkins came to Boston and brought his wife with him, who was fallen into a sad infirmity, the loss of her understanding and reason by giving herself wholly to reading and writing, and had written many books. . . .

The word'll do that, all right. It'll wrack the world, wring it, wry it, turn it inside-out and outside-in. It'll speed it, slow it, set it aspin, it'll thin the air and thicken the water, darken day and gay the night. It'll craze you, the word will, and long before you die, it'll kill you.

lxxv: Billington was executed at Plymouth for killing one. . . .

One what? one servant, or, if servant himself, one master? one wife, one Indian, one Saltonstall, one holier-than-thou, some clerical son-of-a-bitch? or was it one boy who might snitch about their sport in the woods?

xc: At Ipswich there was a calf brought forth with one head, and three mouths, three noses, and six eyes. What these prodigies portended the Lord only knows. . . .

The cow knew too. They portended a cockeyed run on her tits.

36

Thomas Morton, 1590(?)-1646

AN INFAMOUSE AND SCURILLOUS BOOKE

*written by Thomas Morton of Cliffords Inne gent, upon tenne
yeares knowledge and experiment of the Country*

Bradford scorned it from A to Zed and rightaboutface to A
again, it was full of lyes and slanders, he said, it was fraight with
profane callumnies—but more than the book, he scorned the
unclaine bird who'd penned it. A petiefogger, he called him,
the layabout of sundry gaols, the very lord of misrule, and a
screed from such a one was fit to fill but a single need, a wiper
for an ass.

As to the man, little came to light in Bradford's time. His
name was nearly unknown and his father's even more so, and he
went before the Bar in silk—thus far fact. But still secrete are
his place and date of birth, his means and ways, his every-day's
round, wherefore if the claim he laid to *gent* was just, his word
alone is left to prove it. There verity, there fire, ends. The rest
is rumor—that he pursued the law "in the west countries" and
that "upon a foule suspition of murther" the law pursued him.
Take smoke and fire, and you have Tom Morton, inditer of
New England Canaan, that infamouse and scurillous booke, so
full of lyes, so taint with slanders.

A three-part thing, that opuscule, and with one and two there
are few who'll quarrel. They tell in plain phrasing of the
prestance and praxis of the Indians, their divinities (animal in
the main), their holophrastic language, their seemly traits and
comely form (he never saw, the author said, a clunchfisted
Salvadg); one and two, they praise the beauties of the newfound
land, tick off the trees that grew there, the beasts, the fish, the
feathered fowl, they vouch for fruits and berries and such
commodities as marble, minerals, and aromatical herbs, and
there, in that pair of parts, mention is made of virtuous waters,
widely deemed sovereign for barrenness and melancholy.

Part three is the bird of other plumage. There, in that third,
the scribe discovers himself as an instrument of mischief,

37

mocking the word of God and men who went in godly walks, there appear his litigious bent and schismic tenets, clear there his innermost aim, to talk sin and inflame the sinner. Good Lord and good lack, but that Morton was born in Numbers, a prick in the eye of Israel, a vexing thorn in the side!

Thus of the book to come, but how of the man now here? Had he not led settlers to spend their substance on sack and aquavitie, often to the tune of ten pounds' worth in a morning? Had he not sold pieces, powder, and shot to the Salvadges, to the peril of Plymouth? Had he not set up a Maypole at Merry Mount, where the lewd ran rigs with squaws and stooped to the bestial usages of Rome? And did he not debase many servants with such revelry, cause them to drop their rags and besoms and chase after whores in the woods? What had he not done, that one, and what was still in store?

Shyster, rakehell and runnygate, seducer of dunces, nose-thumber, stink on the New World air—he simply had to be taken care of. They sent out Standish (Capt. Shrimp, as Morton called him), and Standish brought him in, their prick, their thorn in the side, and they gaoled him till the first ship sailed for England. He was gone when the tide began to ebb—Avaunt! they cried, and he was gone. He was scriving that book of his before the *Paragon* (was it?) or the *Little James* was hull down to Quincy Bay, and he'd be back one day, grown old by then in wickedness, and with him his triune tome, brazen-bold, abandoned.

Bradford would have a word or two with God about granting fair weather to a ne'er-do-well, Heaven instead of hell for the voyage. "Where were Thy tempests, Lord?" he'd say, "where Thy foundering blasts from the blue?" And God, if He chose to answer, would answer so, "Elder, thou has read the Writ ill; thou hast misread Jesus."

John Eliot, 1604-1690

THE MEDICINE-MAN

We never had a bad day to go preach to the Indians all the winter. Praised be the Lord.   —John Eliot

... He brought us a book, which we were taught to call *Up-Biblum God*, and in that book, he said, there dwelt the Word. Whereupon we sat in a circle and invited it to speak, but if it did as bidden, it made no sound, and what tale it spun we never heard. It had spoken, we were assured, and what it had said was this: that God had made the world, made sky and fox and flying bird, made sun and moon and man, begun with nothing, we were told, no straw, no stick, stone, or strip of bark, and made it all between six dawns and six darks. We were much marvelled that he should so believe. Every red man knew, and red child too, that Manabozho, the Great Hare, had built the world from a single grain of sand, and, more than this, built it on the back of a tortoise. ...

In the photograph, his tomb seems to float, to go no deeper than a leaf would go into the layer of snow of the day or night before. Still unsoiled, the fall glints in the sun as it must've done through all that pristine preaching winter in the woods. No one can be seen in the picture, but footprints have been made since the storm ended, and they wind away toward an iron fence, flaws in the brilliance, dents in the glare. Along the trail, headstones lean as if studying sign: what schoolboy was here, what bull on a beat, what latter-day witch, what Delilah made the tracks in the snow, what sober clerk or sodden rounder—or are they those of Algonquin shades, specters shod in pacs?

They lean, the headstones, as though construing the snow near the tomb. In its black and ancient air lie the nail and hair of a parish preacher, his entrail dust and phalangeal bone, a set of buttons, a sprinkle of minerals, but once, long ago, he'd been a lower-case christ, a refractor of Light, and he'd shone the Word on heathen. The headstones lean, as if scanning the spoor of spirits in the snow beside his grave—Wampanoags, they'd been, Naticks, Narragansets, all now as dead as he.

It'd been love's labor, his three-score years in the Roxbury pulpit, his journeys to the Praying Towns, his winters among the wigwams in the pines; love's labor, his learning to speak a language that was spoken only, that was gone with the going of its sound; love's labor, a gift of the heart, his fourteen years at rendering the Writ into an unwritten tongue and then teaching the unread to read it—but in the end, he'd known the ravishment of asking savages *Who shall redeem you from sin and hell?* and having savages tell him *Jesus*. That book he'd wrought in his sweet love of God, it'd been the Bible in Indian! The headstones lean, as toward some tumult around the tomb, an uproar of phantoms—hosannas, hymns, the Lord's Prayer from wraithlike braves. *Nushum kesuqut*, the stones might've heard—*Our Father which art in Heaven....*

Beyond the paling of the burialground, a legend on a sunstruck building reads *Kornfield Pharmacy*. A place of tobaccos, herbs, powders, pounded roots, philtres—the place of a medicine man. Had it been Kornfield, then, who'd called on this cold assembly, this spalled grave...?

Capt. John Mason, 1600-1672

A BRIEF HISTORY OF THE PEQUOT WAR

Owanux! Owanux! which is *Englishmen! Englishmen!*
—Capt. John Mason

It wasn't much of a war—a single encounter is all it amounted to. One of the Mathers called it *the fight at Mistick*, a day's work, it might've come to, and yet before the day ended, seven hundred Pequots were slain, shot where they stood or cooked to a turn as they fled through blazing brush and burning grain. *Owanux! Owanux!* they cried as they smoked and died on their headlong run. Of the English, only two were killed and

40

twenty wounded, though some few, wrote Mason, fainted by reason of the weather's bite. *Here we may see the just Judgment of God*, he said. *Thus did the Lord judge among the Heathen!*

It must've been amusing, the way flame flushed the Indians and then caught them on the fly. It must've seemed a novel game, a new sort of chase, and great the hue and great the cry as fire coursed like a pack of dogs. They ran, says the Captain, *as Men most dreadfully Amazed*, and it must've made lively telling on the green and in the ordinary, how the savages went to their smellsome maker cured, charred, red meat done up brown. It must've been thought fitting that seven hundred imps of Satan were sent back hot to hell.

For a brief war, a brief history. It was twenty-one pages in all, after which a one-page Addition (*I shall add a Word or two by way of Coment.*) recounting such marvels as these: John Dier was shot in the knot of his kerchief, which, being about his neck, averted hurt; Lieut. Seeley was struck in the eyebrow, but, the arrow turning downward thence, there was no further harm; and lastly, Lieut. Bull was saved by a bite of cheese that stopped a flint in feathered flight. *Was not the Finger of God in all this?*

Père Paul Le Jeune, c. 1635

OF SORCERY AND SMOKE

the two great torments I endured among the Barbarians.
—Père Paul Le Jeune

they said
Blackrobes, people that have fallen from the sky
Because, coming from afar, where the day begins
To fly on the blue wings of the sun, you were
Wrongly dressed for the journey, wearing thongs

On your necks, as if you were your own captors,
And skirts, as do our men that we use as women,

                                        and they said
Blackrobes, laden with odd trifles oddly named,
Censers, which emit a foul smell, and drawings
Of *Jesu* from the side, an offense to Algonquins,
And the crossed sticks that you call a crucifix,
And *reliquaires* (do we pronounce it correctly?)
Containing splinters, bone, and locks of hair,

Blackrobes, we talk in the tongue you taught us,
Hoping that you will not laugh, as we at you
When you tried to convert us in our Montagnais,
For in truth, to provide amusement, we cheated
In the lessons we gave in return for French.
Knowing no words for *Him* and His *Hail Mary*,
We palmed off those we use for other things,
And when you made to tell of hell and Heaven,
You harangued us about our women's breasts,
And in seeking to tally the torments awaiting
Such as we with a sweet tooth for dead Iroquois,
You told off instead the scalps you took in bed.

Blackrobes, we confess to that, but that is all,
And if we league with the powers of darkness,
With their Prince or other and less potent imps,
We mean to keep our treaty secret, as you yours
With your own Oke, the sideway Son that says
The Indian is damned and the Christian saved.

Blackrobes, we make a better medicine than you,
For our land of Death is a place where all go
When they die, the long runner and the thief,
The craven and the brave and the in-between,
And with them go the only goods they prized
When they lived, their weapons and wampum-belts,
Their pipes and pelts, their kettles and rings
(Such things being needed there), and at night

42

Shades hunt with shade bows and shade arrows,
And then, as we do here, they chant and dance,
Or, that world being near this and not at war,
They visit us or we them, and we feast well,
Brave, squaw, child, and dead and living dog,
For dogs have souls, and they dwell with ours.

Blackrobes, your magic is the master of wonders:
When you make books speak, when you charm clocks
(And when at a hand upheld, they chime no more),
When fire can be grown with a gleam of glass,
Or steel and stone, when you dine on Christ,
On the pone of His body and His red-wine blood,
All of us marvel at the range of your dominion.

But, Blackrobes, stranger is the sway you lack:
You kneel and it rains, you pray and it stops,
A miracle of witchery, yet, as no Indian does,
You intervene between an Indian and the fire;
And, sick, you suck medals, and pains go away,
But you are late at portages, and we wait
While you sign the Cross and, singing poorly,
Say *ourfatherwhichartinheavenhallowedbethyname*;
And you sprinkle holy water on profane infants,
Thus turning "little savages into little angels,"
But unaware of your trespass and our anger,
You wear wide and hindrant hats in our canoes;
At your Masses, we hear much blowing of wind,
Mouth-honor, we call it, and we practice it not,
Thanks among us being spoken without sound;
And you beseech us to take only one wife each,
But we have women to spare, and you take none;
And you preach the wrong of eating our enemies,
Though you deem it meet to eat your own God;
And we are rebuked for the fault of immodesty,
Of making public show of our private parts,
But our view, which you have yet to understand,
Is that nothing is private, not we or the earth;

And, last, we know more of good and evil than you
That say evil, if done for God's glory, is good.

Blackrobes, if evil is good, good must be evil,
And your Heaven being the same as your hell,
It follows that your God and your devil are one.
We prefer to believe that the Great Hare made all
And, more, made it on the back of the Tortoise
With mud the Muskrat dove for in the flood. . . .
But you, of course, may believe what you choose,

they said.

Increase Mather, 1639-1723

AS ONCE TO ISRAEL

Methinks I hear the Lord speaking to New-England.
—Increase Mather

He was so christened, it's said, for the great and divers
additions wherewith God had lately favored the country. But
having conversed from the first in Latin, he soon recast the
name, became Crescentius Matherus even before Harvard
enrolled him, and he but twelve years old. The lamp drew him
early, and he felt it to be but a middling day whereof only
two-thirds smelt of the wick. At eighteen he preached his
maiden sermon and at eighty-four his last: in the long
meantime, he penned some nine score screeds, astringent all of
them, importunate, ardent, dire. In one of these. . . .

He said the ire of Heaven—hell—was well on the way,
coming fast and due any day. Indeed, already in view was God's
forked fire, and even now could he hear His tonitruous tone, as
of clouds in collision, clouds made of stone: *I had planted thee a
right seed,* the thunder said; *how then art thou turned into a strange*

44

vine? Heed, New-England, he warned, redeem thy ways!

Give over, he prayed, the Staging of Plays, a naked frivolry, a pastime ateem with turpitude, verily a pomp of Satan, pernicious and apostatic (*vide* Salvian, *De Gubernatione Dei*, Lib. 6.), the aim of which was to fall all Christians away from Christ. Witness, he implored, the calamity of Alipius, that very hopeful young man who, upon attending a Sword-Play, was so much taken by the sight of blood that straightway his mind grew inflamed, as if he had drunk of wine, and besotted he stayed until God laid hold of him. (*Vide* Austin's *Relation*, Lib. 6., Cap. 8.)

And Dicing too he clapperclawed, and Sitting at Cards, and all such Games of Hazard. They were but the casting of lots, he said, a lusory use of the power and name of God. They were heinous, therefore, and the gamesters carnal, and he reproved practice and person with great severity, citing the strictures of Clemens Alexandrinus and Cyprian, of Martyr and Danaeus, and of a certain Mr. Fenner.

To these reprobations, he added a testimony against yet another prophane custom of New-England, the making of New-Years gifts, or *strenae*. This was a paganism deriving from the giving of vervain gathered in the groves of Strenua, a goddess. Jerome, he said, had reprehended this usage as an heathenism, and, in *De Idololatria*, so too Tertullian.

And he inveighed against Candle-mas as an allotheistic thing, a burning of tapers to Februa; and he indicted the vanity of Shrove-tide, with its cock-scaling in honor not of Christ but Themistocles; and he was harsh on the head of Circumpotation, which is to say the Pledging of Healths, a mysterious and papistical ceremony treated of by Matenesius in *De Ritu Bibendi Super Sanitate Magnatum*.

But his best-fledged shafts he reserved for the Nativity and those who observed the day. When Christ was born, he said, no man could certainly say, nay, not the exactest of chronologers, not Scaliger, nor Lidiat, nor Calvisius, not Sphanemius or Parcaeus or even Mr. Perkins. The providence of God had wisely hid such knowledge from his children. There were many

45

who sincerely supposed the true date to be the 6 of January. Epiphanius was equally persuaded of the 5 of January, but there were five Epiphanii, and the evidence is unsatisfactory. Paulus de Middleburgo, on weak grounds, nominated the 26 March, while Temporarius plumped for the 22 May, on or very near. Hospinian, however, made it quite clear that the day was unknown and ought not to be further sought for, since it had had its origin in idolatrous festivals (*vide De Origine Festorum Christus*), and thus all celebrants were but Masters of Misrule. . . .

He died too soon, Crescentius Matherus. If he'd had more time, he might've outproved Hospinian: he might've shown that no Savior had arrived at all.

Nathaniel Hawthorne, 1804-1864

AD LIBS
BY A FICTITIOUS CHARACTER

Child, what art thou?
Oh, I am your little Pearl!

—Nathaniel Hawthorne

As Mr. Hawthorne says, the first thing I saw was the scarlet *A* on the breast of my mother's gown. It was a nearby brightness in a gray-green world, and it drew me as any other would've done, a red flower, a red bird or berry, or fire as it played. It was there at the start, and it stayed, as much a part of Hester as her eyes. But Mr. Hawthorne seems to have been unaware of the second thing I saw, a strange lack since it was a second *A*, this one black.

I was three months old at the time and in my mother's arms on the pillory, pilloried too, the fruit of her sin and therefore no less vile than she. All Boston had come to view us, and faces paved the market place, paned the windows, grew on trees.

There was an absence of color in the crowd—the uniform garb was black—but a certain conical hat seemed somehow blacker than the rest, and so too a certain cape that fell in folds and flared, and I stared at the shape my father thus made: a sable *A* on a sable field.

I seemed to know him at sight, though I've never known how. He stood among the crowd, concealed by it, as he thought, like a shadow lost in the shadow night, but there was my begetter, the black letter *A*. Dimmesdale! Mr. Hawthorne says I touched him once (it was at the Governor's, he claims, and I was going on three), but if so, I must've done it to test whether one who looked so dead was still alive. His eyes were deep in his head, bits of sky in a well, and his hair lay senseless, nonconductive, and his skin was dry, like slough. If, as I said, I touched him once, let it be known that once was all, but quite enough.

My mother must've touched him too, and not his hand, as I did, nor merely with her cheek; it must've been some other member that she reached, sunless, sallow. Mr. Hawthorne describes the result of that collision—I, a wild and flighty elf named Pearl, an airy child, the friend of weeds, sticks, rags, and the *ferae* found in the forest. He dwells long, Mr. Hawthorne, on the wrong they worked on me, but mum's the word on why. How could she have borne him bare, how endured that prying candle, that tallow finger in her private hair? and where, in what field did she lie, what pine-bough bed, to what rock was her fall revealed? and did she cry aloud when his small flame singed her, did she pray when he came or wait till he went? Ah, the reverend Arthur! Pale psalmer, scratcher of itches, charmer of skirts, snake in the pubic grass—what did she find in his leached-out phiz, what soul sat behind those rank clothes, what imbued his sour stuffing?

To my mind, she sinned only in sinning with him. It was her affair that she chose to be ridden, and I didn't care where the rider took her, on the run or standing still or during a swim in a stream—but to receive such a one and make him my father! to couple with that quick-spent dip, that one-cent wick! my God, to be lit but once and then so dimly! And thereafter, for seven

47

years, she wore the badge where the world could see it, while he sequestered his in his room. It was not enough that he carved it with a whip, it didn't matter that it bled and festered and appeared to glow in the dark: he let my mother alone be stoned by eyes.

Mr. Hawthorne says that she took me overseas when he died and, after a span of years, returned without me, and rumor ran that writings reached her from time to time, some wearing seals of an unknown bearing, and that monies made her late days easy and paid for the slate over her bones and Arthur's. But with no blood of my own, is it likely that blood would wed me? With no name but Pearl, would I be apt to flash his ring and bring to bed some belted earl, would I become My Lady, would I be called My Lady Pearl? Or would I, so to say, lie below nobility and sell what Hester had given away?

Edward Taylor, 1645-1729

HOW FAR FROM THEN FORETHOUGHT OF

Lord blow the Coal: Thy Love Enflame in mee.
—Edward Taylor

For three hundred years, his rhapsodies were wrought in private, they were their own heat, their own light in the dark, and now in part they're known, and they warm the cold of other rooms, sparkle other dark—the priest's is one of these, and it glows, as if, with his heart of dust, he feels the blustered coal, knows the preacher's fire.

Roger Williams, 1603-1683

MARK THEM
WHICH CAUSE DIVISIONS

O! how dimme must needs eye be, which is bloud shot with that
bloudy and cruell Tenent of Persecution....
—Roger Williams

They hanged the witches and let him go who might've been their master—a very prince and pimp of weirds, he was, and yet they let him go. The hags they hanged, goody, shrew, and scold, brewer of linctures, stewer of herbs, old sibyl with the age-old labial itch, that kind got their skirts tied and their necks tied too, and no more did they ride flabbergasted faces through the night, no more their triple tits, the fits they brought to pass, the ass they showed to Salem when Salem crossed their road. The one who all but summoned them, him they let go free.

They should've swung him instead of that hellbent crew, made him fly or try to tread on air. Their torment was he, not necromantic charms and curses, devilish hindrances, the vomiting of pins and nauseous pudding, or spells that spun their wits. He was their spear in the side, their crucificial nail, and gladly they'd've scragged him if he hadn't been a gent. They gave the matter thought, though, the driven who'd learned to drive, the burned who'd taken to fire—they mused, they moused, they used the bodeful books, but at the last they turned him loose: he'd been a Cantab in Milton's time, a protégé of Coke's.

Themselves compelled in old England, in the new they held with duress—victims there, here they victimized. *For dyvers newe and dangerous opinions*, their sentence read, *the said Mr. Williams shall departe out of this jurisdiccion*—they churched him with their civil power, expelled him into the wilderness to dwell and die outside the wall. Beshrew the day! It would've been better to kill him, still his tongue, take his quill away. They'd live to rue the fifty years they left him of his life.

Banned from the church, he was meant for hell, but never did they understand that in sending him, they'd sent themselves: they the fried and he the fryer, and for well-nigh half a century, he kept the fire hot. They were church and state in one, he said; the hats they wore for the Lord were those they wore on the Bench. And he said their trend was over-the-mountain, and the end of their road was Rome. And this he said, that there was a cloud on their title to the land—a red cloud, he said it was, the color of an Indian. And he found virtue in all manner of people, the Turk, the Jew, and the poor, but he found none in war, he said, none in tithes, forced oaths, and mortals who were in on God's unerring truth. They'd cried for mercy once, he said, and now they denied it, they'd decreed that all must read with *the Cleargies Spectacles*, they'd smelled out thought and straitly wrought such ruin as *no Uncleannes, no Sodomie or Beastialitie* could equal. Persecution! he said—there was the bloudy tenent that would never wash white!

They lived to regret that he lived to be eighty.

Jonathan Edwards, 1703-1758

HEAVEN WAS HIS COUNTRY

All who are truly religious are not of this world.
— Jonathan Edwards

It was early his country. At twelve, at twelve!, he wrote of flying spiders and their silk balloons, the riders of the sky. *One would think they were tacked to the vault*, he said, and he watched them spin down from the trees and glide on the wind away. And he drew them too, the wondrous little beasts, drew the twigs they pended from, the gossamer ships they spun, their ways of casting off and sailing ablaze in the sun.

He made a further note, that they were borne never away from the sea, but ever toward it, there, as he supposed, to perish. He must've pondered that fate. At twelve, at twelve!, he must've thought of parables. The power to levitate between earth

50

and heaven—was that not a faculty of man as well, was it not
given to man to choose between hell and grace? Parables
enacted, he must've thought, the living truth, the truth *shown*.
Not spiders were they, blown against their will. They were
men, and they had chosen—at twelve, at twelve!—and they
were riding toward the Fall.

John Peter Zenger, 1697-1746

THE WORLD OF MOVABLE TYPE

To Subscribers who take my weekly Journall—Gentlemen,
Ladies and others: As you last week were Disappointed of my
Journall, I think it Incumbent upon me, to publish my Apoligy
which is this. I was arrested.   —John Peter Zenger

If the charge had been illiteracy, he'd be jailed yet. He'd seen
little schooling in Bavaria, where he hailed from, and none in
New York, where he went, but (or because of which, who
knows?) he chose to become a printer. He did himself small
good at the trade: he was a dunce in the new language and an
ignatz in the old, and that Journall he ground out once each
week seemed likely to leave him unrenowned. All the same, he
made the Pantheon, that printer who couldn't spell. He doesn't
belong there, of course, he stands around as if he'd rung the
wrong bell, opened the wrong door, but he's remembered, the
unlettered man of letters, and his Whiggish betters are dim or
forgot.

He was an April fool for them, the Palatiner. He was their
cull, their greeny, and when they barked at the Crown, he bit
for them, whereupon, for publishing their sedition, he was
thrown into what he called *the common Goal*. Bail was set at ten
times his worth, one pound for every florin, which compelled
him to sit on his bung for well-nigh a year. They sprung him
finally, those he was a handle for, and if they ever wondered

51

why he hadn't betrayed them, they laid it to his wooden wit: he was a dumkopf, a gaper, an eater of flies.

It's said but not certain that he lies in Trinity yard, but wherever they put him when dead, from there the four winds bear word that he made the word free. He didn't know he was doing that. He thought he was selling his Journall to Ladies, Gents, and others.

Sam Adams, 1722-1803

THE YELL OF REBELLION

The People shouted, and their shout was heard.
—Sam Adams

A brewer's son, Sam was, a low line to come from, to some even sinful, and they threw a stone or two, their way of showing bluer blood. Sam the Maltster, the swell-born called him, Sam the Publican, and as for his Sons of Liberty, they were Cromwell's spawn!, which is to say they were Sons of Bitches. Scurvy fellows, that kind, scum, vagabond strollers, smell-feasts, malaperts, swillers of flip, and levelers one and all—Publican Sam and his jackanapes from the *Green Dragon*, his "Loyall Nine" from the *Bunch of Grapes*.

Boston Latin didn't change matters, nor yet four years at The Yard—he was still a lout, a bottler's get, and for all his skill in the dead languages, he was quite unread in the living, a know-naught, he was thought to be, and he'd risen forty before he could see past the salt. By then, he was casting the two-way shadow of failure, a black one behind him and a blacker one ahead.

He'd tried his hand at banking, but for him money loaned was money sent to hell, and as a merchant, he'd known not when to buy nor knew he, alas!, how to sell, and in the end, he'd even blown in the brewery. Voted in as Tax Collector (he who couldn't pay one!), he came up four thousand pounds short, seven, some say, and no one knows to this day whether he made good or stayed shy. He never turned an honest groat, that Sam, and he wore the news like a sandwich-man: his coat was rusted rosy, and there was paper in his shoes, and with the palsy coming on, he was out of his prime before he was fairly in it. A life was nearly over that had never quite begun—but at forty, God damn it, Sam began to live!

He got himself a quill (he must've stole it from a goose), and he was on his way to prying the Colonies loose from the gents, from the cocks and capons sent slumming by the Crown, the court-plastered bastards that spat on the riff and raff and other dogs. He'd learned to write, Sam had, and he burned with words—ah, he could scriven birds from the sky, bring them down on the wing. Such was the venom of Serpent Sam that he had merely to touch the shadow of a flying thing. . . . *The People shouted*, he wrote, but it was Sam shouting, Sam all the time.

Tithing-man Sam, how rum that the plum of all the world should fall to you, thief, liar, firebrand, Mohawk chief, gammoner, pasquinader, mob-raiser, topsy-turvy bass-ackward rack-and-ruin Sam! What days they were, with the blooded rich in flooded britches and the hinds kicking their fulsome behinds! How odd, how odd, to find the bottom on the top! *Sam had shouted, and the shout was heard.*

But just as odd and even odder, that when the shouting stopped (See the Seven Articles!), all was the way it had been before: the top was on top again, and the bottom was the poor. It would take another war. . . .

53

James Otis, 1725-1783

NEAR THE GRAVE OF PAUL REVERE

*I hope when God Almighty shall take me out of time into
eternity, that it will be by a flash of lightning.*
—James Otis

They say that he too lies in the Granary Ground, but would
bones be found under his stone today and the bones if found be
his? Who would know now? His life was dogged by some
chance-medley that expunged his traces, covered the places
where he might've made a mark, sponged the slate, stranding
him with dates of birth and death and no certainties in between.
His papers, letters, pocket-books, all were lost, sown in the
roads and blown away, borne off, burned, and toward the end,
his brain ablaze as well, he became spleeny and skittish, a
container of heat, and he began to misspell his name. He died of
the fire within him and the fire that fell from the skies: in an old
steel engraving, you can see the lightning strike him yet. He got
his wish—he went in one bright celestial gesture.

Only indicia remain, like minims culled from a blast, the
charred scrap, the fused coins, the swatch of scalp and hair, but
whose details they are none can swear to, except maybe Paul,
nearby Paul Revere. He survives in reports of his presence, in
secondhand accounts of word and deed—there's something
about a screed of his against the Writs of Assistance, something
about the tyranny of the Stamp Act, a note on damp tea, a book
he wrote on Latin prosody and another he did on Greek—
rumor all, street-speak, like the tale of his whaling in an
ale-house, when he was hit on the wits with a cane. (*My friends*,
he's said to have written, *my friends think I have a monstrous crack
in my scull*).

His friends were right, but somehow, whether he's fact or
figment, he seems to belong here, hard by Sam Adams, among
those who fell in the Massacre, a step or two from Revere. The
bits that persist, the letter or letters, the hearsay—from the
foot, we may judge of Hercules. He was mad while the war was

being fought, but when that bolt sought him out, maybe it cleared his head, maybe he knew we'd won just before he was dead and gone.

James Madison, 1751-1836

THE VIRGINIA PLAN

The great desideratum in Government is . . . to controul one part of the society from invading the rights of another.
—James Madison

From the windows of his room at Fifth and High, he could've seen the State House steeple through the rain; it was only a square away, situate among some elms and girt with graveled walks, and he could've seen, inside the wall, where flowering shrubs in hummocks lay; he could've seen it all from where he stood, with his back to a fire, small, for it was May. But within the reach of his eye, he saw nothing but images imagined: he saw rained-on roads that led from near and far to him, to here.

A slanting day, he may have thought, grained with rain and gray, and through it, more through mass than rain-shot air, many men were on their way, some by sea and stream and some by fluid road. With their arrival, there'd be fifty-five all told, and beneath the steeple he was staring past, they'd sit or sprawl in a great chamber and debate the shape of an uncreated world. Some were only names as yet (who was William Few, he may have wondered, who were Blount, Houstoun, Spaight?)— names, he may have thought, but he knew that in the weeks to come, he'd have to see to more than designations: he'd have to treat with minds.

The rain fell, some of it down the chimney, making the fire flare and smoke, but he was unaware of rain or fire or Philadelphia: he was dwelling on those minds and how to make them meet. Loosely tied, thirteen sticks had the strength of each, not the strength of all, and what was true of sticks was true of jurisdictions—but would Jared Ingersoll agree, would Jacob Broom and Caleb Strong? Bold and brazen rebels, these, but did they know of Shays and real rebellion, or did they suppose him merely a rifler of arsenals, a Massachusetts thief; were they warned and wary now, or, secure in fief and chattel, were they nodding over wine? If the last, they'd awaken to find their decanters gone, their tenements taken away, they'd find the poor paper-money rich and the rich being told where to dig.

A coach passed, leaving transient tracks in the mud, and as he watched it run toward the *Indian Queen*, he wondered who was aboard—was it Rutledge, was it Randolph in the rain, was it one of the Pinckneys and which, the Cotesworth Charles or Charles the plain? What would they say when before them lay his plan for their keeping much by giving some away? Would they spread the vote a smidgeon thinner, would they allow the mob a lower house and bank on banking its fire from a house that was higher up, would they see the virtue of one-for-all and the vice of all-for-one?

Who had come in that coach, he wondered, Carroll of Carrollton, Davie, Clymer, Mason, or was it someone he'd never heard of, coming in someone's place? The rain was constant, and it striped the air. He thought of the *Indian Queen*, and going to the door, he bade his man (Sawney, was it?) to cry him up a chair.

Thomas Paine, 1737-1809

THE BONES OF A PAMPHLETEER

*inflated to the Eyes**

His ship, the *London Packet*, was sixty-three days raising Cape May, but long before that he was down with the putrid fever, and he had to be carried ashore. He must've been scribbling as he went, though, because in no time at all, as Atlanticus, or Aesop, or Vox Populi, he was addling our wits with words. Why did we suffer his rant, and why, when we saw the side he took, did we fail to cook his goose? We were none of his greasy business.

He was English, not exactly a foreigner, like some God damn Swede or Turk, but foreign enough in the whiggery he managed to work with his reed. We'd done a bit of leveling on our own, of course, with token bones for bottom dogs, but nothing to take the top dogs off—and then along came this nobody that none had sent for. He'd been a staymaker, we were told, and he'd sailed with a certain Captain Mendez aboard a privateer, and as an exciseman for the Crown at fifty pounds a year, he'd gauged the weight and worth of merchandise and tallied pipes of wine. He was a nobody, from a long line of less, the sort due to be buried in an only coat and short a pair of pennies for his eyes; his grave would wear till it wore away, and, dead, he'd be a button or two and a minim of something that once would've bled.

We let him stay, and he wrote his head off—and it was touch and go whether he'd do as much for ours. We managed to keep them, but he cost us the Scepter, and now, for want of a king, we have to rule by seeming to be ruled. But what will happen when we run out of bones . . .?

*and big with a litter of revolution**

He was a drunkard, we claimed, and brandy his drink, and the stink he gave off would empty a room. He had the Scotch fiddle, by which we meant the itch, he was awkward, rude, slovenly, and slowcome, a slob, in brief, yet oddly vain, and though his style was coarse and his grammar bad, his pen was for sale, and well it sold. He was a little mad, a fellow-lodger said, and the thief who stole his bones called him base. He was blue-balled with a love-disease, but so far as one wife knew, he did no more with his member than draw it when he pissed.

---

*Gouverneur Morris writing of Tom Paine

They're dispersed over England now, those ghouled bones of his, they're lost, those that weren't tossed to dogs, they're gone, the ones that weren't gnawed, forgotten, or flung away: somewhere a skull's asquill with matches, and somewhere else phalanges are strung to jig in the wind, and ribs, like fallen vaulting, lie haphazard on some floor, but they bear no name, the relic ruins, and none can say they once were Paine.

Thomas Jefferson, 1743-1826

REBELLION IS
AS THE SIN OF WITCHCRAFT

The mass of mankind has not been born with saddles on their backs, nor a favored few booted and spurred, ready to ride them. . . . —Thomas Jefferson

When he showed up in those days, few were the hats to be thrown in the air, and fewer the flowers that fell in his road: neither high nor low could square him as their own. The demos never quite knew him, and the aristos knew him too well, wherefore in exquisite places or among the crass crowd, he was merely spoken fair and, with some token civility, soon allowed to pass. All told, it was small wonder that none could say where his heart lay—with his kind of blood, was it?, or whither it was sent by his mind.

A gent he was born, or as much a gent as others aplenty, which is to say he wasn't sired in a ditch or dammed in a stand of corn: his mother was a Randolph, and she came to the bridebed *comme elle faute*, with two hundred pounds in hand. A high enough beginning, Tom's, and just as high his end. In between, he wore dago britches, whored with half-white slaves, bought books, artware, fiddle-gut, and those precious stones of wine, the rubies of the Rhone, bought, bought, all his life he bought, horses, harpsichords, mechanical dingamaree, and when he

58

wasn't measuring fences, he was eyeing someone's wife. Aye, Tom was high, for he could speak with ease in Latin, dream the *Iliad* in the Greek.

But even so, to fellow elegants, he had something common about him, and that something was more than the mere *grocerie* that he'd gotten from his spear side. The cotton hose he wore, and the torn and soiled clothes, the love of acquisition, the fear of being taken for a scrimp, base such things and baser these, his palter in the face of crisis, the pell-mell way he fled from Tarleton, the mock he made of Christ (the French infidel!), and finally, and more than all, there was that weakness of his, a vulgar craze for lore.

Where had his learning led him? Rider born, he bled, said he, for the ridden. He rode with anguish, his boot felt each kick it gave, his spur felt its galls, he rode saddle-sore in spirit, he whipped against his will, he cried aloud at wrung withers and slobber strung with blood, but bred to ride, he rode, rode till the day he died. The blues were dubious, the rubes doubted too—and so the hats, all but a few, stayed where they were, the wall was given him often, and through a soft and courtly murmur, he went along his way.

Did he know what he was after, the buyer of things, the courtier, the keeper of slaves, the writer of fire- and time-resistant phrases, did he know his real, his unrevealed aim? Did he care for the jade or the seat he sat on its back . . . ?

John Marshall, 1755-1835

A CASE
THAT WAS NEVER TRIED

*Let the end be legitimate, . . . and all means which . . . consist
with the letter and spirit of the Constitution, are constitu-
tional.*   —John Marshall

THE CASE

THEM *vs* U.S., 1 Cranch 136a (1803)

PRESENT:

John Marshall, Chief Justice, and William Cushing, William
Patterson, Samuel Chase, Bushrod Washington, and Alfred
Moore, associates,

Levi Lincoln, Attorney-General, for the Government,

Lincoln Levi, for the Plaintiff-Appellants.

The opinion of the Court was written by Marshall, Ch.J., and
by him read:

Plaintiffs come before this tribunal on a writ of certiorari
from a ruling of the Circuit Court for the 2d District.
Application had there been made for an order requiring the
defendants to show cause why the Constitution of the United
States should not be declared unconstitutional. After exhaustive
argument, the order was denied. We think it was rightly
denied.

The gravamen of the plaintiffs' cause may be summarized as
follows:

> —That prior to the founding of the Republic, the
> thirteen colonies were the property of England, private
> titles therein being held subject to the pleasure of the
> Crown;
> —That independence from England was achieved
> through a common effort of the people, thereby
> transforming Crown property into public property,
> owned in common and in common to be enjoyed;

60

> —That the Constitution, in failing so to declare and provide, became illogical, or, as learned counsel for the plaintiffs puts it, *lusus a non lucendo*.

Mr. Levi's Latin is not before us for review. His reasoning is, however, and we find it repugnant.

To us, all property is private, and none more so than government. It does not belong to the people, that great beast *fruges consumere nati*, that two-legged thing born, as it thinks, to consume the fruits of the earth. Government is vested solely and of right in the rich, the able, and the well-descended, or, more simply said, in the few. To such, which is to say, to us, the populace is merely meat, a low form of lukewarm life, and no man of blood, wit, or wealth would consort with it lest he become its kind himself.

Mr. Levi seems to cherish a singular delusion: that the Constitution somehow resulted from a chance meeting of transients in the city of Philadelphia in the month of May, 1787, wayfarers whose ways had fortuitously crossed. Nothing could be further from the fact. The five-and-fifty men who came together where and when they did were delegates certified by their several states to join in the drafting of a national compact adequate to the exigencies of independence. Chief of these was assuring that those who had set the feast did not partake of it.

It was not to be endured that to the plebes should go the delicacies of this world, the cates and the kidneys, the larded snipe and wines, wherefore those fifty-five were told. . . . But they did not require to be told. Surely Pierce Butler, from the Duke of Ormond's line, did not require it; nor did William Davie, rich enough to pony up $5,000 for a horse; nor did Jonathan Dayton, who had bought a million acres in Ohio and paid the government with its own continentals; nor Alexander Hamilton, who, while bulling the market through a partner, bulled as well the partner's wife; nor one with so sweet a name as Daniel of St. Thomas Jenifer; nor John Langdon, who bragged of buying 6's at 7¢ on the $; nor did Robert Morris need telling, he who'd financed the Revolution and along the way himself. Verily, in the midst of war, the laws are silent, or, as Mr. Levi is aware, *inter arma silent leges*.

All such, and the Pinckneys too, knew that though a man might be a reasoning creature, men were unreasonable. Singly only were they able to think; in the pack, they simply slew. Few, though, dreamt of a crowned head; there were other things to be tried before trying some home-grown George. One of those was a device that would seem to change much yet keep all in fact the same, a trick to make dogs suppose they were running while their masters knew they were leashed. When perfected, that device, that trick, would be called a Constitution.

Mr. Levi urges now that we sweep it away, but we fear he has been too long at the lamp and too little at the window. Writ there in public places, on walls, on tombs, on coins, on carriaged faces passing by, is the tale of man's most durable love, the love of having, or, in Mr. Levi's native language, *amor sceleratus habendi*. The few always knew that love, and the fewer, they believed, the better. The fifty-five agents they sent to Philadelphia did the work of damming up the demos with seven articles and a preamble. Let the work stand.

The judgment of the Circuit Court is affirmed, the application is dismissed with prejudice, and costs are assessed against the plaintiff-appellants.

All concur.

J.H. St. John de Crèvecoeur, 1735-1813

LETTERS FROM AN AMERICAN FARMER*

We have no princes for whom we toil, starve, and bleed: we are the most perfect society now existing in the world.
—J.H. St. John de Crèvecoeur

. . . God forfend I should content myselfe with speakeing well of the countrie as it is and make no mention of the daungers looming. May my penne fall if I tell of what the eye hath seen and suppresse the apprehention of the heart. To all seeming, the visible America is a flourishing boddy, hale, vigourous, durable, nay, perdurable, as though it had thryce imbibed from the eternal founte. Would that so firme a boddy were as sound within! Would that it harboured not the worme!

A paradize, this land, a heaven on earth in truth, in truth another Garden, but it suffers, alas, of the ills of the one before: there are no heavenlie men. As in that realm eastward of Eden, so it is to the west. Here too each is but an Adam, aproned against his nakedness and hidden in the cool of day, here as there the thorne and thistel grow, and bread is braken in sweat, and wet too the herbes. Aye, our Adams have eaten of the tree, our Adams have been beguiled. But there is a greate and fatal difference: the first man sprange from the Lord; the late one springes from man. To this pleasaunce, this Kingdome Come, he came in sinne, thieving, and having stolen his share of the whole, he will steal still more and kill to keep it, steal from fellow thieves, more and ever more, till some own all there is, wax fatte while others wane, and all the smaller serve them. . . .

---

*The authorship of this fragment has never been established. There are some, however, who ascribe it to de Crèvecoeur, in which case it would appear to have been intended as a note to his Letter III, entitled *What is An American*.

AH SINFUL NATION

May 14th, 1804: This spot is at the mouth of Wood river, a small stream which empties itself into the Mississippi, opposite to the entrance of the Missouri....
—Meriwether Lewis

From there, it was four thousand miles to where he meant to go: the mouth of the Columbia. Most of the journey would be upstream and uphill, and Indians would bar the way, and weather, and God Himself with His godless acts of flood, fire, and the bloody flux, all these and more to cap the usual grind, the ups and downs of a living day. A far cry would the party go before the going was over. It got off to a late start and made but four miles on that mid-May afternoon, and yet the men were of good cheer, being four miles nearer the Pacific four thousand miles away.

In the pass of time, they sailed by willow islands, caves, and rocks inlaid with colored flints, and ashore they found inscriptions, buffalo tracks, and sweet and salted springs. A well-favored land, it was, deep in grass and timbered too, with grapes and other fruits abounding, some, like the Osage plum, supreme in size and savor. They took in that region raccoon, a number of deer, and a bear, and one of their hunters told of having heard a snake make a guttural sound not unlike a crowing bird.

From the bluffs at the riverside, raspberries impended, a red rain that fell as they passed beneath, and pelicans were seen, and parroquets, and paccaun trees, and the men saw nuts on the buckeyes, saw honeysuckle and wild rose, and on one of the boats a whippoorwill rode for a while. And flights of swans flew past, and wolves were descried, and wild rye dipped in the winds and rain. Many isles or aits were in the stream, some so dense with berry-vines a mouse could scarce have gotten through. And now cottonwoods were found on the banks, so called for the coma around the seeds, and once a starving dog gave cry from the bank, and though the men fed him on the fly, he would not follow further.

The hunters brought in turkeys, geese, and a beaver, the last of these alive, and some became attached to him and soon made him tame. A camp of Ottoes being met with, presents were exchanged, the Indians giving fruits of the tree and vine and receiving a flag, medals of the second and third grade, whiskey, and a canister of powder, and they were perfectly satisfied. The mosquitoes were very troublesome, but the air grew clear in a violent squall, a heavy fall of rain.

Where the current ran close to shore, late or soon the bluff would crumble with its stand of trees, and these silt and sand would fill to make half-sunk snags whereon many a twig was a snake. The very stream was a snake, so writhen that in nineteen miles of flow, only nine hundred yards were gained. In that country, the smallpox had been, and there were Indian towns where the malady had frenzied the people, and to end their suffering, the men had burned their women and children and then themselves.

Where beaver had dammed a creek, the crews composed a drag of bark and willow, taking a store of fish of many kinds, among them pike, bass, trouts, red horse, perch, and the like, also mussells and other shelled food, and these, with some ducks and plover, provided a welcome change. But one of the sergeants, Charles Floyd, was seized with the bilious colic, and all care and attention being ineffectual, his strength failed, and he died, though not without seemly composure. He was buried with the honors due a soldier, and a cedar post was placed to mark the spot.

And now herds of buffalo were seen, and birds of the plains, wrens, larks, and gentle martins, and there were multitudes of prairie dogs, or barking squirrels, and there were antelope, fleet as the flight of time, and brant eclipsed the waters, and every copse was stiff with deer, and there were sweet plums for the picking, and prickly pear, and red currants, and rue, and there were timothy and other grasses, and trees made stockades along the stream. . . .

And thus it went for two more years on river-road unnumbered and street newly made by their feet. No wires staved the sky, and no sign said Jesus saved or *EAT DRINK BUY*. There were snows in store, and falls of frozen rain, and there were heights in the way and flood and fire to be passed, and, last, there were Indians. But there came a day, after many and many other days, when they reached the end, which was the beginning again. . . .

> *Sept. 23rd, 1806: We descended to the Mississippi, and round to St. Louis, where we arrived at twelve o'clock, and having fired a salute went on shore and received the heartiest and most hospitable welcome from the whole village.*

In the grand national open drain, America flows past. Its brown sap goes by, and its skim and scour, and in a churn of crumbled counties, the bones of De Soto tumble another time. Snags turn over and rest for the rest of the year, and from the Kaskaskia and the Wabash come sand, feathers, the scales of fish, and flakes of shale—all this has mingled with the stream, and rust, spit, piss, and a two-masted shingle launched on the Cumberland (as what—slaver, yacht, or privateer?). And leaves spin in color-wheels of engine-oil, and Lovejoy's type is in the current, and the intestinal blood of Père Marquette, Ojibway hair, and the salt of tears shed for dead Ann in the Sangamon, and a piece of the True Cross still sails with a fleet of other splinters, and the fingernails of niggers roll, and swollen dogs, some of these white—all this makes the undrinkable drink, the Mississippi.

Ah sinful nation . . . The cormorant and the bittern shall possess it.

Susanna Rowson, 1761-1824

CHARLOTTE TEMPLE,
a tale of truth

But ah, the cruel spoiler came—

—Susanna Rowson

Among her pages, fact and figment wind, a wreathe of myth and actual, and you wonder whether Charlotte lived or floated through her mind, and the spoiler, you wonder, did he breathe once and wither what breathing touched, or was he merely something written, someone to be read. But no matter—he came, you're told in the story, when scarcely fifteen summers had shone on Charlotte's head, and before another knew her, the strayed one was dead, a shade in the yard of Trinity. Her stone has fallen on its back, and grass has overgrown it, vagued it at the edges, and it seems to lie displayed on plush. It wears no date or boss, only the good name lost to Montraville.

(or Montrésor, as he was known in life, forty years of age, wed and well so, with ten children and a wife, a Royal Artificer, the word in his trade for Engineer)—Montraville or Montrésor, one knave or the other, or both if the same, put Charlotte to shame and laid her in the grave. And then away and home to England sailed Montraville the fiction or Montrésor the real, and with him went his fistula and his dreadful hydrocele—ill now, the cruel spoiler, and in the cruel hands of the Sisters Three.

Well, there's the tale, true or otherwise, the article or a dream adrift in a dream. But it's all one to Charlotte, a long while lying below the pointed pile of Trinity, a bearing once for ships and birds, a pharos they saw from the sea. It's hidden now, the spire, sunk in the risen city, and the ships and birds steer by higher things. Only at meridian does the sun find the deep-down steeple and the ground around its feet; only then do the headstones warm and the dead arise, and Fulton's soul joins Gallatin's, and Hamilton's and Charlotte's stroll.

Davy Crockett, 1786-1836

COCK-FIGHT AT NATCHEZ
or, why the Colonel went to Texas

In the state of Tennessee, they come in one size only—big.
—Col. Davy Crockett

Note: The work called *Col. Crockett's Exploits and Adventures in Texas* (1836) ends with an entry dated March 5. Scholars have long surmised, however, that other memoranda were added before the Alamo fell on the following day, and with the discovery of material suppressed for over a century, their speculations become fact. These pages, lately found among the effects of Charles T. Beale, who edited the original manuscript, are here made public for the first time. They complete the March 5 entry and continue the Journal to what must have been almost the very moment of the final assault on March 6.

March 5 (cont'd.)

... I am back to my scribulating. There was a little disturbment outside, but it is over now, and about twenty members of a Mexican surprise-party lie dead as jerky. Your sarvant and old Betsey, we are liable for three such, one of which we blown his head clean off of his body, but him being on the run at the time, he kept on doing so, and, Aye God!, if the varment were not firing away as he ran. I given him my best grin, the kind that used to would fetch a coon from a tupelo tree, but I misforgot that the dago could not see it, and I had to hamper him by stumping off his trotters at the knees. May I be stobbed, though, if he did not reload and fire one last shot afore he fell. . . .

There was a hoosh in the night, and then, clear and pretty, came a trinkle of trumpet-music, silvery-sweet, like drops of melt from the moon. Ah, but it was not a surenade. It was the *Deguello*, the Fire-and-Death call, and it meant that no quarter would be given and that all of us soon would die. I suppose I could spend this last allowance of time the way the others is doing, praying with the praying kind or just studying the dark for day-up, but I'll be damned if I pray and condemned if I

68

don't, which is why I chosen to light this candle-end and write down the whyforness of me being in this tremenduous and lonesome place called Texas.

I am here, I do not doubt, because the Big River is a movable and wandering thing, a regular she-sarpent, and where she was when you looked before, she wasn't when you looked again. That's the whole how-so of it: I was headed for N'Yawlins, but the keelboat ran aground at Natchez-under-the-hill, and I have lived to rue the day. Aye, if that broadhorn had not of found bottom there, I would not of wound up here. I will now factify the sarcumstances that led me to this primary.

Well, sirs, they purely tried to free that ark, but she was stuck for fair, and what she'd need was a spate of rain, and there being no more use to stay aboard, I cut the fool and went ashore. After a spell on the stream, dry-land life seemed kind of slowcome, so I looked me out a dram-shop where maybe I'd sagashuate better than I was doing in the sun. I've lived to rue the day.

Dram led to dram, alas, and in no long time I was standing on one laig and crowing like a cock. "I ain't had a knock-fight in a month," sez I, "and if I don't get salted, I'm going to spile. I'm the most ramstudious creature the Lord ever made, and when He seen what He done, He set down and cried. I'm vemonous," sez I, "and I'm touchous too, and if I ever get the underholt on Old Harry, you'll hear a hellaballoo. I'm half man and half salamander," sez I, "but having four halves, I'm also half horse and half Sagittary, and with a dash of dragon and a dob of wolf, I only piss once a year, but when I do, I piss pure blue wring-jaw. And just let me be proud," sez I, "and the women had better hide, because I get taller than tall timber and as wide as Tennessee. Yea," sez I, "where I hail from, our ticklers come in one size only—big."

I stopped there for another dram, and that was the one that undone me. Over in a cornder, there was little puny sort of man, all warpen and wiltered, he was, streng-gutted and unsubstantious, and when he spoken, which he did, he sounded high and thin, like the nippers had slipped, and he got trimmed instead of the bull. "You're a tellsome man, Colonel," sez he, "but I didn't hear nothing that made me waxy save the last.

Being a York stater and knowing our powers, I vow that you would not be top-cow where I come from, no more, maybe, than you are right here."

Well, sirs, a brace of squirls could of sat on my eyes. I pushed them back in the sockets and stared in furiation. "Warpen little man," sez I, "except I have been badly fooled by my friends, York state is not yet in the Union."

"It is in the Union," sez he, "and what is more, it is filled with men each of which wears a set of prides that would shame the rest of the nation, espeshually Tennessee."

I flapped my arms a couple of times, because I had it in mind to fly. "York state man," sez I, "I'm a natural stone-horse, and no mistake. When I am on the big road, I stomp both sides at once and turn up a furrow in the middle."

"That's Tennessee talk, Colonel Crockett," sez he, "and Tennessee is famous for woppering words and teenchy do."

"York state titman," sez I, "what do I have to do to make a Nazarene out of you?"

"You have to perduce the article," sez he. "Unsight-unseen, it's just another little Tennessee pinky-finger."

"Piss-willie," sez I, "you are about to see a tallywag that was thousands big when I was borned, and it ain't done nothing since but grow."

With that, I brang forth a swingeing dingle-bob that made many a man think his eyes were lying, and it didn't just stay there, scratching the floor. It made for the door and reached out for the river, where, I declare and swear to God, it shoved that flatboat back in the drink. "It's your turn, York stater," sez I.

I knew I'd met my match the minute he unbritched. Out of that black straddle of his, he unquiled the most calamitary dick-nailer of a pezzle ever wore by man or dingmaul. It didn't just go for the light, it took the wall with it, and it wasn't out there no time before a logger with a team tried to snake it away. It was one snatching fine cadulix, and so said all Natchez, which stood there cravenating it. I was a disgraced man, and I snuck away to this destructuous place, to Texas. . . .

March 6

The candle's about gone, but it don't matter, because the sun's coming up, and they're playing that Fire-and-Death call again. They'll be here soon. They'll put me out of my misery. . . .

Paul Bunyan, c.1837

LEGEND WITH ADDED MATERIAL

What a noble logging land is the He Man country!
—Paul Bunyan

Trouble with Paul was, he had the big head. He got it from knocking over all those Michigan saplings, and before long he was thinking he could do the same to everything made of wood. In Michigan, maybe, but not in Oregon. You ever hear the story?

He come out here a while back to make an estimate on a logging operation, and he no sooner seen his first stand of Douglas fir than he said, "I guess I should've brung m'lawn-mower." That didn't go down quite like he expected: nobody laughed. We just stood around waiting, and I'm here to say that when an Oregonian waits, he can outwait the Final Judgment.

Paul couldn't take that long to show off, and after a week or so, he said, "Well, what does a man have to do to get a 'Gee-whiz!' out of you Modocs?"

We kept on whittling, and he got sore, and taking out a jackknife of his own, he grabbed the top of the nearest tree and said, "Y'know what I'm going to do? I'm going to snip this sprout clean through the butt!" and *slaunch!* he made a cruel swipe at that fir. A long strip of something peeled back over his fist, and he stuck out a finger to stop the tree from falling. Nothing fell. What'd peeled off was a layer of the knife-blade.

"Must be that diamond-wood I hear about," he said, and

71

strink! he took another slash. That time the blade broke off and flowed away red-hot. "Hard stick of wood," he said. "Wants to be drug out by the tail." He got a good holt—only one hand, of course—and he give an honest tug. The tree didn't budge enough to shake the smell off it. Paul was owly-eyed by then, and he tried to hide it by saying, "Must've lost m'balance," but we noticed that when he clapped a fresh grip on, he was using both his graspers.

We'd heard that when Paul really fastened onto a pole of wood, it begun to ooze, like he was squeezing cheese, but this one, he couldn't dent it enough to make a weevil uneasy. With both arms around the butt, he foamed and faunched till Oregon spun twice counterclockwise underfoot, but nothing else moved except a stream of pure block-salt down Paul's back. He looked bad.

We were still waiting for something out of the ordinary to happen, and finally Paul put on a silly sort of grin and said, "No damn hands at all," and down he knelt and went to work with his chewers. He gnawed for two hours and a half, but all he had to show for it was a hogshead of tooth-tartar. Somebody let out a laugh.

That was all Paul had to hear, and cupping his hands, he bellowed, "Babe, come on out here to this unnatural state and bring m'private ax!"

He must've used two lungs—before the echo died away, the Blue Ox was in from Michigan with the ax in his mouth. We moved in a little for a look at the tool, and there's no denying it was the finest double-bitter ever made. The blade'd been tempered in a forest fire and a tidal wave, and the cutting-edges'd been ground so keen they only had two dimensions, and the helve was one whole petrified hickory.

"I'm just going to use the flat of it," Paul said. "That'll be sharp enough." And *squinch!* he swang. The side of the blade cut a hole in the air that hasn't healed yet, but that's all it did cut, and a couple of people yawned. "Oregon's sure hell for rusting tools," Paul said. And *splinch!* he swang a second swing. All that happened was, that ax-head puckered up like a bottle-cap and fell off.

72

Paul laughed, but the laugh was so full of hollow that there wasn't any room for the sound to make a noise in, and it come out silent. "Only been horsing all along," he said, and he turned to the Blue Ox. "Been saving this weed for you, Babe. Push it over and let's get on home."

I'll say this for Babe: he was ready. And I'll say this too: he was willing. But that's all I'll say, because he wasn't able. He set his poll against that fir, and he shoved so fierce that his hind legs passed his forelegs, and he had to move backwards to go forwards, and all of a sudden he quit moving either way and sat down. Paul rushed over to see what the matter was, and it didn't take him long to find out. "Hernia!" he said, and he laid down and started to cry.

Right then, the sun skipped four hours and set in four seconds, and we were about to go home for supper when a voice come out of darkness so dark you had to light a match to see whether the match you just struck was lit. The voice said, "You ought to call in another man, Mr. Bunyan."

Paul stopped crying long enough to roar, "No other man can do what I can't, and if he could, he'd be me!"

The voice said, "They tell some pure things about a natural man from down south."

"Can't none of 'em be true," Paul said. "There never was a southern man could work his way out of his mama's belly."

The voice said, "The one I got in mind has quite a name down home."

"Local boy," Paul said. "Couldn't heft a boxcar."

"That's no lie," the voice said. "I'd tip over. I got to have one in each hand."

"*I!*" Paul said, and he sat up. "That means you're talking about you!"

"Name's John Henry," the voice said, and then the darkness moved aside and got out of the sun's way, and what we seen was a nice-looking colored lad dressed in a fresh suit of overhalls. "Pure proud to know you, Mr. Bunyan," he said.

"By the jowls of the Great Hog!" Paul said. "A junior eight-ball!"

"A Negro," John said, "and a natural man."

73

"Natural man!" Paul said. "Just how old are you, son?"

"Eleven, going on twenty-two."

"Holy Ham Hock! You ain't even learned to count yet. For your benefit, *twelve* comes after eleven."

"That's Michigan-counting," John said. "I don't grow a year at a time. I double."

"How many birthdays you had so far?"

"One."

"You trying to tell me you was eleven years in the stove?"

"Naturally," John said. "I'm a natural man."

"Well, you ain't going to look so natural when you get back to New Orleens," Paul said. "Put up your feelers and square off!"

"I don't want to fight you, Mr. Bunyan."

Paul's lip curled back so hard that his teeth curled with it. "I thought you was black," he said, "but I guess you're a colored boy of a different color."

"Oh, I'm black, all right," John said. "I'm a natural black man."

"Black, nothing!" Paul said. "You're as yellow as a quarantine flag."

"I was brung up not to hit a old man."

Paul got madder than God ever did at Old Horny. He swole up like a toad, and he kept on swelling. He pumped rage through his system till his hair split nine ways and knotted itself like a whip. He began to sweat live steam, and he ground his grinders so hard that his spit turned to glass, all the while stomping with such power that he made footprints through his calks. He sure looked put out.

"You're black," he said, "but that's only a crime in Dixie. And you're just a pukey boy, but that ain't a crime nowhere, only a misdemeanor. But you don't have respect, and that's a felony even in hell. I hate to do it, son, but I've got to learn you better, so wrap yourself around something and hold on tight: I'm going to put the clouts to you."

Paul snaked off his belt, and while he was taking a few practice-swings, the black boy walked over to that troublesome fir, and without so much as a wheeze, he yanked half a mile of it out of the ground. Paul was dumb-struck.

74

"It's in kind of snug," John said, "but it ain't pure stuck," and again he pulled, and another nine hundred yards of timber came up.

Paul put on his belt again. "Typey type of tree," he said.

"It ought to be rooting out real soon," John said, and now he fell to drawing the tree up hand-over-hand, like it was a fish-line. But the more that came out, the more there was left, and the going got worse all the time. The boy took to unscrewing it, and that helped for a while, but it wasn't long before he was sweating water in sheets, like plate-glass. Paul swabbed him off with his shirt, but when he come to wring it out, it was bone-dry. "I don't sweat *out*," the boy said. "I sweat *in*."

But now the tree wouldn't even unscrew. The boy tried it first one way and then the other, and it seemed to be jammed for fair. He lost his temper, and drawing back, he cocked a fist and threw it at the contrary trunk: it only went in elbow-deep. "Like a little old peckerwood!" he cried. "I must be losing my natural power!"

"Listen," Paul said. "I been measuring this wood you've tore up, and it comes to a good seven thousand miles. If that's losing your power, you ought to be glad. If you had it all, you'd kill yourself just by staying alive."

But all the boy could say was, "Only eleven years old, and I'm losing my power!"

"You ain't *losing* it," Paul said. "You just ain't *got* all of it yet. When you're full-growed, son, you'll move the globe without a pry."

Well, Paul might've been no great shakes as a logger any more, but that was a fine remark even for a has-been, and it pleasured the boy. "Maybe you're right, Mr. Bunyan," he said. "Here I been thinking all along I was a natural man. I guess I'm still only a natural kid."

"And kids get wore out," Paul said. "I just wanted to see how long you'd last."

"I still got some kid-power," John said. "Now, if I only had some man-power to help me, I could fall that tree yet."

Paul teetered, looking up at the sky. "There's quite a few

75

men around," he said. "Pick yourself a good one."

"How about you, Mr. Bunyan?" the boy said.

"Shake, Mr. Henry!" Paul said, and they shook.

At that, they joined hands around the tree, with Paul saying, "Count off, somebody. At *three*, we pluck this stick like a straw from a broom."

I hadn't counted that high for a long time, but I took the chance.

"One . . .," I said, and they closed in tight.

"Two . . .," I said, and they got set.

"Three!" I said, and they made a muscle.

They must've made more than they meant to, because it boiled out of their arms like lava and flowed away smoking. They put so much pressure on their legs that the kneecaps wound up behind the knees. They took in air so fast they had to breathe in and out at the same time. And then the tree began to give!

There was a scraping, gnashing, cracking, tearing noise— and *thunk!* out came that fir like the world's cork. We all felt a draft and looked down. At our feet, there was a hole straight smack through to China! It was like Paul to go and pick the one tree the Chinks had planted upside-down, and it sure put the kibosh on him.

Or didn't it?

Washington Irving, 1783-1859

IN THE KAATSKILLS

Even to this day they never hear a thunder-storm of a summer afternoon, but they say Hendrick Hudson and his crew are at their game of nine-pins. —Washington Irving

It would've been better not to wake. It would've been better to sleep on, dead, deep in that glen where the Kaaterskill rose, and the bitterns hid, and the watersnake sunned when the sun

76

was overhead. It would've been better there, where none came but the queer conjured crew of the *Half Moon*, and they but for a day of nine-pin thunder every twenty years. It would've been better to stay, to lie forever between two wales of dust, one a bygone gun and one a keg of Hollands, without a dog, without a wife, himself dust and by all forgot.

He wasted time well once. He built fences for others and let his own stock stray. He fished in the rain and fowled in the shine, and though weeds grew and slates fell, time went by on a one-way tide. He flew kites for children and told them tales of witches, ghosts, and the Iroquois, and their lurchers knew him and suffered him to pass. He ran errands for the village wives, never wondering who odd-jobbed for him, and holding it better to starve on a penny than live on a pound, he laughed at those who wound their watches.

Now some new do-nothing flies the kites and spreads the fictions, and some new pack trails him on his back-door rounds. There are new wives and new errands now, and new hounds drowse while time ticks by. Even the old Rip is new. Gone the free favors and the love of child and beast, gone the squanderer, sowing the hours where they yield the least. He has learned to think, and to all who'll listen, he sells his story for a drink of gin. He kills no time now: he's like the many, and time is killing him.

Ralph Waldo Emerson, 1803-1882

DOES THY BLUE EYE

ever look northward with desire . . . ?
—Ralph Waldo Emerson

A short-lived line, his Ellen came from, the breast complaint, they had, and she too bled from time to time, before they were wed and through their year or so (is that all there was?) of union. She was less than twenty when she died that winter's day,

77

and thereafter he was often descried—every morning, some say—wending toward her grave. What drew him, what he did when he got there, what made him have the box dug up and opened, what he thought then of the grayed face, the offwhite clothes, the stiffened curls, no one knows now or, knowing, brings to light.

In her album, he'd written a phrase for her in French. *Friendship*, it told her, *is love without wings*. Did he fly a little, you wonder, in that sweet short year, did he look southward with desire, or did he, as he'd do for another fifty years, walk on that occasion too? Was hers the only blood in the twain, did she stain for both when her lungs tore—in her own fire, did she burn for more than one? *L'Amitié est l'Amour sans ailes*. Was he merely an embalmer, a drainer of others and drained himself—is that why he'd unearthed her, to inspect his work, to see how a love he'd cast in French had lasted out the year . . .?

Henry Wadsworth Longfellow, 1807-1882

THE JEWISH CEMETERY AT NEWPORT

These Hebrews in their graves. . . .
—Henry Wadsworth Longfellow

Their stones, that look like those of Moses, floor the shade of Touro *schul*: below them old fleers of the fire but old ashes all the same, Jews dead on a later pyre and as far as ever from the milk-and-honeyed land. They touched him, the exodists, they caught his heart, and he must've marvelled that his kind could've turned from the Way, hated and spurned them: a Second Coming, he must've thought, was the one He owed to these. They wrung him, that people who lived as they read, from the right, they caused his tongue to speak.

78

Francis Parkman, 1823-1893

HE CALLED HIS RIFLE *SATAN*

My thoughts were always in the forests.
—Francis Parkman

Nous sommes tout sauvages, the Iroquois carved on some ruin they'd made—We are all savages, their blazon said—and though he read the phrase to embrace Indians alone, they may have meant the race of man. *Nous sommes tout sauvages*, they scrawled in blood or spelled with bones, whereat he held them to be a lower breed and mixed as well, mongrels leading mongrel lives, thieving, fickle, feculent, void of pity, raptured by the smell of gore, the sight of pain. *Nous sommes tout sauvages*, they roughed out on some stove-in boat, some half-burnt wall, and he took them at their seeming word: the Five Nations were savages all. They warred endlessly, he wrote, even on the dead, their women whored in the open, coupled at a glance, and common too were bed and board, the latter comprising such vile aliment as roots, bark, buds, offal, and their enemies. They drew rudely, he deemed, and they practiced tattooing, coiffed their hair in grotesque fashions, and, on the turn of a painted plum-stone, gambled weapons, raiment, wives. Sickness came from sorcery, they thought, and sorcery, more preposterous!, was the cure. Vain, he called them, boastful, grasping, unmalleable, a greasy people that crouched like apes, and as for their gods, good God, they were beavers, they were turkey-cocks . . . !

He had the same bent, a craze for blood. He never owned cat, dog, or bird, but always somewhere about him there was a dead rat, a broken snake, a limp something he'd blown loose from its life as it flew, swam, or ran. He shot raccoons, chipmunks, buffalo, and frogs, and at sea, it's said, he tried to bag a turtle. He slew at will, carried *Satan* till he was too old to aim it. *Nous sommes tout sauvages*, the Iroquois cried, they who could write but little to him who read that little wrong—and the night before he died, he dreamt he'd killed a bear.

Edgar Allan Poe, 1809-1849

IN BRONZE ABOVE A DOORWAY

Little home of a great poet
— 13 West Range, University of Virginia

Did I live that life, the one just over, those forty years of dayless days, and did I behave as they say I did, were such my ways, did I write the hack and consequential work I signed, did I wear black to match my blind-man's view of the world, a worldwide open grave, was such my turn of mind? Did I stem from strolling players, did my father cut and run and my mother die of lungs, leaving a few ringlets and a miniature, so poor, so poor she sang and danced in motley till a month before the end?

Was I given a home by Allan, and did he give or I take his name, was I clever as a child, did I rhyme in Latin, recite to guests for praise and watered wine? Did I love at fifteen, my first time and my first Helen, and was she soon insane and dead and I insane alive? Was it then I began dwelling on tombs and cinerary urns, on magical radiances, compelling perfumes, ciphers and fascinations, dark-age horrors, death gradual and intricate and sometimes by machine? Did I know of drink then or learn its use at school (milk slings, they say I took, and peach-and-honey—what was peach-and-honey?), and while there did I lose three thousand at loo, debts of honor (whose?) that Allan refused to pay?

Should I have starved when he cut me off, was it base to enlist as a common soldier, a loss of face to eat my country's bread in the ranks, and if so, why when appointed to the Point, did I dram it till they drummed me from the Corps? Didn't it matter, didn't I care, did I guess at twenty-two that there'd be no forty-four—those sudden tirings, the troubles in my head, my shaking hands, and where was all desire except when desire was safe, among consumptives, among premenstrual misses and no longer bleeding maids?

Why did I marry my twelve-year-old cousin Virginia, whose

mother was nearer my age, and in the hovels we shared with a
cat, a bobolink, and a pair of canaries, did I ever see her naked,
did I surprise secret skin and shocking hair, and did I sink the
sight in opium when drink was slow to drug me? My aunt
(Muddie, I called her, and my bride was Siss), my kindly
tireless uncomplaining aunt, did she beg for us in shops and on
the road, did she take in laundry, mending, lodgers (and lodge
them where, on what part of the floor?), and when I went away,
did she tend my wife in her lifelong dying and send me the fare
to come home?

Did we move from place to place, we three with cat and
birds, always to a smaller space, always taking fewer things, and
if, as the doctors said, I had a lesion of the brain, explain my
presence at the Springs while Virginia bled the bedsheets red?
Did I lift material, pretend to erudition, puff jinglers for puffs
in return (*R.H. Horne puts Milton in the shade*)? Did I laud
empty lines, woo lady poets with reviews, give them valentines,
was I not myself, was I high cockalorum when Lowell came to
see me, did I court the widow Whitman and still unwidowed
wives? Did I rave in my drunken manias, did I take poison and
puke it back, did I, that winter at Fordham, warm my virgin's
feet with her cat?

Tell me, did I die in the street or a Baltimore room, and tell
me lastly this—some day, somewhere, in bronze above some
lintel, please God will it say *Domus parva magni poetae?*

John Woolman, 1720-1772

A SMALL FIRE

I have seen small fires in long cold Storms.
                                        —John Woolman

He would never dine from silver, never drink of wine: it was
stained, he said, imbrued with the blood of slaves. Nor would
he wear dyed cloth, for dye would hide the soil, and it was meet

81

that man should be sweet and cleanly. And he forswore gain, it being the cause of war, nay, and more, it was war itself. And it was wrong, he held, to vend strong drink except in seemly measure, wrong to lend at seven per cent, wrong to abuse the land and misuse horses. *I have often felt the motion of love,* he said, and he did feel it, felt it all his life.

How he must've bled, then, when he penned that Bill of Sale! The buyer was a Friend, the seller the same, but that which went from hand to hand was no stand of wood, no sack of grain: it was a black she, a fellow creature, man. How he grieved for her, bought for a certain number of coins (blood-fraught silver?), how he agonized! *I have often felt a motion of love,* he said, and he felt it then, when he did as bidden, sold a living soul. But did he not marvel at the evil hold on his pen?

Phillis Wheatley, 1753(?)-1784

AH! WHITHER WILT THOU GO

Thou who dost not daily feel his hand and rod
Darest thou deny the essence of a God!
If there's no heav'n, ah! whither wilt thou go.
— Phillis Wheatley

She was a black, stolen in Senegambia when but seven years old and !sold! in Boston, remembering of Africa nothing but the way her mother had poured out water to the rising sun. A tailor bought her, Wheatley his name, and she soon became his eye's apple, and he let her be a Wheatley too and taught her how to read. Taught well, for at nine she knew the Scriptures and was wise, it's said, in astronomy, history, and dead and living tongues, yea, she spoke Pope's stylish Homer and Vergil's stately feet.

At fourteen, she began to write and wrote (having encountered an atheist) of the daily feel of the rod and hand of God. She knew more than the unbeliever did: there was One from whom all things great and small did flow; her theft at seven had been willed in Heaven, and the same was so of her exportation in a shipload of shit, her sale to the Boston tailor, her pretty tricks with heroic couplets. Such things had been Caused, and the Cause dwelt there, on high, wherefore when that scoffer loomed, she said *Darest thou deny!*

What she couldn't say, being still a slave, was that there'd *better* be a God! There'd better be something Supreme, or simply something, to explain why she, black daughter, was there in Boston and her mother somewhere else, pouring water for the rising sun!

Herman Melville, 1819-1891

A VISITOR
FROM THE *BACHELOR'S DELIGHT*

Captain Delano, now with the scales dropped from his eyes, saw the negroes, not in misrule, not in tumult, not as if frantically concerned for Don Benito, but with mask torn away, flourishing hatchets and knives, in ferocious piratical revolt.   —Herman Melville

When Delano climbed the gangway and boarded the *San Dominick*, he stood on the deck of a blackbirder. He'd seen that kind before, though, and therefore he didn't stare on finding slaves at sea: they were merely goods being taken to market, like pekoe in the tea-trade. Nor did it awaken wonder that Don Benito, a fine-spun sort, seemed drawn a shade too spare, or that, while rich in dress and language, he was less cordial than custom called for: he was Master there, and he might wine a guest or hang him, as he chose. It was quite fitting also that he should be attended by that half-naked little nigger of his, rather like a struck dog in the way love and *please* ascended from his face. Nor was it odd that his fellows went about free of chains: they must've learned from Death that none could walk, none

83

swim back to Ashanti. On the *San Dominick,* all was in order—black at work and white at ease.

The scales never did drop from Delano's eyes: he stayed in the dark the livelong day of his life. He saw nothing on the slaver to sigh for—a bit more bark in its Master, maybe, and maybe a bit more bite, but the list ended there. Nor did he note the queerness in the queer farewell at the rail, nor while waving to his late host from the whaleboat, and to the little black dog at heel. He was still benighted when Don Benito jumped his own ship, when three white sailors followed suit, when the hatchets began to fly, and simians jigged on the cabin roof. He was dead to all but the blacks' revolt, which he read as wrong deposing right: there could be no such thing as a whitebirder.

His mind fumbled with the notion, though—downeasters might be had for ivory one day, and Quakers bought with spice. . . ! Beating off the three clinging sailors, Delano's oarsmen rowed him back to the *Bachelor's Delight*, and there he had the guns run out, and the jigs' jig was up. The black pirates, those that lived, were carried to Lima, altitude 512 ft., and hanged a few yards higher to give them a better view of Peru.

Mark Twain, 1835-1910

GIVE A DOG A BAD NAME

Given under my hand this second day of January, 1893, at the Villa Viviani, village of Settignano, three miles back of Florence, on the hills. —Mark Twain: *Pudd'nhead Wilson*

In the tale as told, two children were born on the same day to the Missouri household of a certain Percy Driscoll. The mother of one was black in a sixteenth part of her blood and therefore, under the laws of the state, black in all eight pints of it. Her son, got by a white father, was black only in a thirty-second part, not nearly enough to dinge his skin or kink his hair, but he was no

84

less nigger than his mother and just as much a slave. *Valet de Chambre* was the name she gave him, after a phrase she'd heard above the stairs, but he answered to something lower-flown: *Chambers* would always fetch him.

The other child born that day came from the groin of Mistress Driscoll, and he was as white as God's laundry, the clouds in the sky; he was white from the outside-in and the inside-out, white from A to izzard and halfway back to A. His name, which his mother was allowed but a week to delight in, a week to speak before she died, was *Thomas à Becket*, a big handle for a little blade.

Chambers and Tom, infant slave and infant master, alike in age, place of birth, and actual color, which was the cameo-pink of canned salmon—both now were fostered by the mulatto woman. They sucked the same pair of tits, they cheesed up the same sour curds, they shiced themselves in the same brown carefree way. On many a spring and summer day, they sat face to face in a toy wagon, gumming bacon-rinds, reaching for sounds, smells, and flash until sleep sank them without warning. They were hard to tell apart. The elder Driscoll could distinguish them only when they were dressed: his own child wore ruffled muslin and a necklace of coral, the other one a tow shirt and no *bijouterie*.

Now to the Driscoll household, hard lines came. Thrice had small sums of money been stolen, the dollar bill, the odd coin, or thrice had they walked away, and on the fourth occasion, the slaves were summoned and told that unless the thief owned up, all would be sold downriver and no two to the same master. All, of course, confessed, the mother of Chambers along with the rest, and for the moment, Driscoll's hands seemed tied. But with danger past, she knew that danger remained. One more loss of loose change, or none, for no reason was needed, and her son might end in some far-south field, a hand, a man named Boy. No long-tether times for him then, no rafting or fishing, no soft touches won by foxing the whites, no slow-speed days, no skim off the *crème de la crème*—and in sudden dread, she switched the halves of the Driscoll whole. The muslin and coral went to Chambers, and the tow smock went to Tom, and together with the clothes went the names.

There were queer consequences. Before the switch, the children had been like as drops of rain; afterward, strange to say, in no way at all were they the same. The great change took place in the new Thomas à Becket, the Valet de Chambre that was, almost as if magic resided in the unfamiliar name. If so, it was evil magic. No sooner did the little slave sit at the little master's end of the wagon than he became odious. Five months old, abruptly he turned spiteful, cranky, and base: a bully, a glutton, a crooked stick, he cried without cause, held his breath and blued, spilled food or threw it away, pounded, scratched, ruled with an iron hand no bigger than a doll's—a nigger doll's.

What did all that, you understand (and made for murder later on), was that dash of black blood, that taint, that tinker's damn, that metastatic fraction, that thirty-second part.

Harriet Beecher Stowe, 1811-1896

THE LORD HIMSELF WROTE IT

I was but an instrument in His hand.
— Harriet Beecher Stowe

Many an abomination has been laid at my door. Every clerk that rhymes on Sunday, every Rialto scrivener, every hack with the scribbling itch—all say that if they've sinned in words, they've sinned as me. Their sprung and stumbling rhythms, their daring dimmed by quotes, their Eureka!s among the known, their slow-motion wit—all declare these doings mine and doubt meanwhile my one Creation.

I didn't write this book, and I didn't use the woman as my fist. The fact is, I gave up writing a long way back, at the height of my powers and ahead of my time. Few read the stones I sent from Sinai and few my writ on the Chaldean wall, and all those few were Jews. Allow me this, though, that I used no blind; the

86

name I signed was my own. Why hide now, then? And with the whole wide world to choose from, why behind a mother of seven, the wife of a crammer in Maine?

Her household smelled of smelling-salts, of six children (I took back the seventh, a year-old boy), of tansy, camphor, bacon-smoke, bound sermons, hand-me-down air, and, still faint and still afar, Bright's disease. I glanced through a window once and saw Mister conning the Scriptures and Missus dashing off a war, and the sight sent me home with the blues.

I never wanted that war (I didn't care a sneeze for the niggers), but she did, and she got it, and some five hundred thousand whites died for a book (in paper, cloth, or cloth full gilt, with discount to the trade). The only book that made more killing is the one that was written about me.

Roger Taney, 1777-1864

THE LANGUAGE OF THE LAW

The court is of opinion, that, upon the facts stated in the plea in abatement, Dred Scott was not a citizen of Missouri within the meaning of the Constitution of the United States, and not entitled as such to sue in its courts. . . .
—Ch. J. Roger Taney

Dred's real name was Sam, and that's what fetched him when he was owned by Peter Blow, not Sam this, Sam that, Little Sam, or Bigger Sam—and when the white man hung it on the Ozark air, the nigger ran like a bugled dog. And so it went till the master was dead, but all that got for Sam was a new collar that read *Now I run for Doc Emerson.*

(Taney—written so, but Tawny for the tongue—came from a line of servants that rose to keeping slaves. His father, in fact, grew quite splendid: he chevied the chase, tossed his pot, faunched in a foam of skirts, and, after a stabbing over some twat, died in a fall from a horse. A more circumspect man was Roger, a pulsecounter, and he managed to live for eighty-seven years, a few too many for Sam.)

There came a day when this Doc Emerson took Sam and crossed over from the slave side of the Miss' to Rock Island on the free. They had a queer kind of air in that place, Sam found, cold and clear and rare, and it let him see the far away, brought it near, like a winter day. He saw more, saw what he'd been blind to before, that collars like the one he wore were not the style in Illinois. He took it off: he caught the freedom itch.

(Taney was related by marriage to *The Star-Spangled Banner*, his wife being a Key, sister of the one who'd been stirred to doggerel by a fired-on flag with fifteen stripes. On the whole, Taney thought it a fair bit of crambo—*gleaming-streaming, wave-brave*—but that phrase *land of the free* was sand in his eye: the scion of servants still owned slaves.)

Aye, he took that dog-collar off, Sam did, but Doc put it right back on, and then Sam sued, and Doc he upped and died. It was ten years before the case made its way to the Supreme Court, and waiting there on the bench was Taney, Ch.J. By then, it was forty-some years after the perilous fight in the dawn's early light, but the sand, the *land of the free*, still galled the Taney eye.

(The gavel fell, and the bailiff bawled *The case of SAM vs THE STAR-SPANGLED BANNER! Draw near, all persons concerned, give your attention, and ye shall be heard!* Sam was no person, though, and he wasn't there. Papers were there, affidavits, caveats, demurrers, and writs, but no Sam. Sam was marking time in the Show-me state.)

The question before the court, Taney said, was whether sucking free air made a free man out of a slave. It stood to reason that the answer was no, Taney said, because where did that free air go? It went inside a slave, into slave territory, you might say, and so far from freeing the slave, it stopped being free itself. In Sam's black lungs, it became slave air, and it would only be free when he was, in the world beyond the grave. Sam was in Missouri, and Taney showed him.

Abraham Lincoln, 1809-1865

A FEW APPROPRIATE REMARKS

Fourscore and seven years ago. . . .
—Abraham Lincoln

You'd not have supposed that such a one could bring such prose to pass. You'd've thought the words would match the maker, a thing of joints and angles, fitful and graceless, insectival, almost, a creation that might crawl or spring but be of the air never even if on the wing. You'd've expected language that went with his skin, a mummy's, it could've been, harsh, dry, integumental, bloodless to the touch. It would trudge the page: there'd be no cadence, no soft footfall, for his metric feet would be flat, and a figure of speech, if found, would've made him a figure of fun, a horse in a hat. He was something more than merely high; he seemed higher than he was, they say, a long six-four, a tree-trunk, a bole of a man with wens like burls in the bark of his face. That was it, you'd've fancied, a man with the bark on, hardly the kind who'd phrase so that birds in flight would light to listen.

They'd've learned from him, those singers, if ever they'd dipped their wings. They'd've heard lyrics that needed no lyre to be sung, that played and sang in themselves, word and string in one. They'd've been fixed by such tones as only the wind had made before, a score arranged by trees. *Fourscore and seven years ago*, he said, "a few appropriate remarks" for the living and the dead in those fields and for the bundles of feathers that perched on the stones.

Henry David Thoreau, 1817-1862

A CALL OF NATURE

*Ask me for a certain number of dollars if you will, but do not
ask me for my afternoons.*   —Henry David Thoreau

He said his say against the peculiar institution, and now and
then he bedded and fed some runaway slave; he gave and
gathered freedom-money, he wrote his share of touchwood
words, and here and there in his Journal, a note throws light on
where his heart was and its shade; he made himself over that he
might remake the world, a perfect one to perfect the many. But
in the end, it came to this, that never was he in danger: he threw
no stone nor had one thrown at him.

Oh, it was a marvel, the way he could reach into a hole in a
tree and bring out a screech-owl—and she with young in the
nest! It had to be seen, his trick of luring fish with his hands,
bream that would nibble at his fingers and let themselves be
lifted from the stream. And mice would come and feed at his
feet, and crows would eat from his mouth and frogs lie supine to
be stroked with a weed, and he spoke the kind of woodchuck
that woodchucks could understand. Birds came and went at his
chirped command, and the same for squirrels and, it almost
seemed, for rain. Flowers opened and closed for him, clouds
appeared and were blown away, and arrowheads grew where he
pointed at the sand. It was a miracle, what the man could do, an
eighth wonder, you might say, like a pyramid, like a hanging
garden, and children had faith in him, as if he were their eyes.

Still, he was never brained with a cane, and no one rowed
across a river to kill him, or towed him through the streets with
a rope, or shot him behind the ear, or broke his neck with the
knot of a noose. He slept well, they say, that one night he spent
in jail, and come morning, he went his way when his bill was
paid by a party in a veil. His aunt, it may have been, but no one
ever knew.

Henry Timrod, 1829-1867

NO MARBLE COLUMN

The shaft is in the stone.   —Henry Timrod

He didn't last long in the gray, or the butternut, or whatever
it was he wore. He had tb. when he put it on, and in a year or so,
he took it off, bloodied from the wound inside, and making
what songs were still unsung, he bled from the lung till he died.
He lies now under the live oaks in a Carolina churchyard,
where, in their seasons, azaleas in white and rose array, and
mimosa sows its yellow dust. He sleeps; he sings no more.

They'll hew the shaft some day, and they'll grave it with his
name and dates and, to contain his short-lived-life, a phrase
about his blameless honor, his scorn of gain. But front or back,
no stone word will speak of what he'd spoken for in rhyme—the
right to own and sweat the black.

Albion Winegar Tourgée, 1838-1905

THE LOST CAUSE

*The South surrendered at Appomattox, the North has been
surrendering ever since.*   —Albion Winegar Tourgée

He never had a doubt as to why the war was fought; it was
fought to free the slaves, for no other reason, and it was dust in
the eye (he had only one) that the Union must be saved. He
didn't care a pinch of owl-shit for a Union where you had to
look sharp to tell which was the nigger and which the mule. He
wouldn't've died for that kind of House—to hell with it! let it
divide! He damn near got his back broke at Bull Run (a
gun-carriage struck him), but he wasn't there to stay the Erring
Sisters, no, sir, only to make them let the black man go.

91

Partly paralyzed, he was out for a year with that sprung spine of his, but as soon as he could walk, he ran: he was a fightin' man. He got to the front just in time for the rout at Perryville, where he blocked a chunk of canister with his hip. From then on, he could've watched others fight, but, no, sir, he went right back in to war some more. Not for long, though, because during when he was out with a forage-party, Morgan's horse soldiers bushwacked the detail and bagged him, along with a goodly part of the 105th Ohio.

He done a trick at Libby Prison, where he read *Don Quixote*, but the old Spic had nothing to learn him. He knew where the windmills were, and when he was swapped for some Reb, he went on a hunt for the man, looked him out at Murfreesboro, at Chickamauga, and in and about Chattanooga, and finally, trying to jump some ditch, he come up shy and fell in, smack on that bum back of his, and the fire-and-death phase of the war was over for him. The rest of it was not over, no, sir.

Not at Appomattox, it wasn't, no, sir, and it was more than ever on when Lincoln was shot. The niggers were still black, and they still couldn't squat on a white man's hole, so he went on down to Carolina, bad back and all, and for fourteen years, he tried to win what Grant had lost. He got to be nigh about everything going amongst the Tarheels—lawyer, editor, farmer, commissioner, judge, and manufacturer of pick-handles—everything but a Southerner, that is, and clear to the end, therefore, he was only a liar, a fool, and an abolition nigger-stealer, lower than his bung in the mire, not quite animal and not quite human, no, sir.

Fourteen years, he put in down there with those Secesh bastards, and never a day passed but what they didn't kill him in their minds. They built him more crosses than they ever did for Christ, and they burned them all on his lawn; he kept three loaded pistols in the house, and one he wore when he rode down the street to the store; he was hated coming, and he was cursed as he went away. That never changed, no, sir.

And all through those fourteen years—first as a lawyer and then as commissioner, farmer, editor, judge, and maker of pick-handles—he tried to equalize those blacks and whites, wrote about it in verse and wrote in prose, spoke in court and spoke in the road, lectured, scolded, pleaded, and what he got for his pains was another round of calls from the Klan while niggers without balls left red footprints on the ground. Nothing came of his fourteen years in another country, no, sir.

It was the same in his own. Ten million words later, or twice ten, who knows?, for the one-eyed soldier, the war ended, but he was still firing when he fell, the old soldier—he was a fightin' man. Yes, sir.

Joel Chandler Harris, 1848-1908

BRER NIGGER

Ef you bleedzd ter eat dirt, eat clean dirt.
—Joel Chandler Harris

During Marse Joel's funeral, there had been a sudden summer rain, but it was over by the time her carriage returned Miss Sally and the boy from the cemetery. He did not follow when she entered the house; instead, he waited for the screen to close behind her and for her steps to fade in the hall, and then, cutting across the yard, he made for Uncle Remus's cabin. Scuffing through the glisten on the grass recalled the grass at the grave, bright against the bare and rain-dark fill, and he remembered too a priest at prayer and a ray of sun as the prayer ended, as though to light the dead man's way. To the boy, these were strange things, but when he told them to Uncle Remus, he thought, Uncle Remus would explain.

At the boy's touch, or, as it seemed, just before his touch, the cabin door opened inward, uttering more than once the only word it knew, but on that day of rain and shine, merely a black presence remained in the cabin; Uncle Remus was not there. His awls and hammer lay on the bench, and his balls of thread and wax as well, and nearby on the floor there were broken shoes to mend, and clothes that hung on pegs seemed to be scaling the walls; on the air, a whiff of tobacco and a skiff of smoke, but Uncle Remus, old black with a Frost of whiskers, Uncle Remus was no more there.

The boy stooped for a skive of leather, and as he turned it in his fingers, gently a voice stirred the curtains of his mind, and he heard slurred warm-taffy speech, and the world of the cabin swarmed again with creatures, peopled, it was, aye, peopled with terrapins and tar-babies, with rabbits in pants and shirted foxes, dupes some of these and some of them witlings, sly, overweening, show-offs all and riding high for the fall to low—but to a man, to a critter, they spoke in Georgia coon, a limpsey flow like honey from a honey-spoon.

And then the boy dropped the scrap of leather, and at once all went away but the geist of tobacco, the ghost of smoke, and though not yet did he know it, from that moment on, the boy was dead. He did not know, not yet, that Uncle Remus was dead too, gone with his maker to meet the Maker of both, he did not yet know, Miss Sally's boy, that he was headed for the Place of Clean Dirt, the only place. He went to the door—this time it did open of itself—and walked toward the big road.

Hinton Rowan Helper, 1829-1909

HAVE YOU ANY WOOL?

We should remember how essential it is, in a flock of white sheep, to destroy every lamb with the faintest trace of black.
—Hinton Rowan Helper

It was on a day of March winds and gray rain that the last of a lifelong spate of words ran down and out of his hand, and with nothing more to say, he calked the cracks of his room and opened a cock of gas. The next morning, a maid found him on the floor—at ten on the tick, it was, as if he'd left a call the night before. The police thought it queer, that towel he wore around his neck, but after all he was old, eighty and more, and maybe he was afraid of taking cold.

Had he died fifty years sooner, noted men would've borne him in slow time to the tomb, and in a minute gun's gloom, a firing squad would've rifled the air. He was a known man then, a nob among nibs, a lone Southerner against the South, a farmbred Tarheel who ran off at the mouth about the harm of slavery. He was at the eye of that particular storm, and some held that his name was apt: he was a helper indeed, for he helped to start a civil war. But he lived too long for honors; he died in the wrong century.

With slavery gone, he showed the true face of his abolitioning: what he'd really aimed to abolish was the black race. They were baboons, he said, base creatures with a head of bone and a back-thrown brain, and they were snout-mouthed, as he put it, and glut-footed (whatever that was), and they stank; there was something odd about their build, and he wrote of their voices as eunuch-toned, as if his ear were attuned to the gelded note. They were God-forsaken, he cried, wherefore he denied them too.

He stayed too late to have mourners, paid or otherwise, and when no one ponied up for a stone, he was laid in a nameless grave. Still and all, a ship would be christened for him when the right time came, a little joke to be played on the monkeys, a monkeyshine, you might say.

Emily Dickinson, 1830-1886

REVENGE OF THE NERVES

the doctor calls it.   —Emily Dickinson

A sickbed phrase, garish words for pallid days, but in his journal he wrote *Bright's disease*. From a long-sunk Anatomy, some bubbles of lore still rose, and on a remembered renal section, he saw the Malpighian pyramids, the columns of Bertin—*Bright's disease*, he thought, and he reached for a pen, but the pen was in his hand and his finding on the page. He knew what was killing her, and he could almost set the time. He knew from the color and kind of urine, from the pains in the back, the fever, the hydroptic hands and feet, he knew from old books, old cadavers—*Bright's disease*.

It was a high wide world, the room she lay in, and the sights it held he never descried. There were wilds inside the wall, there were rare shores and private ports of call, and he strode unaware among flowers, flights of bees, birds achant in a virgin mode. In that world of hers, he breathed love, not air, but what he sought there was Bowman's capsule, and what he found was a name for death—*Bright's disease*.

Rebecca Harding Davis, 1831-1910

LIFE AND DEATH
IN THE IRON MILLS

The idiosyncrasy of this town is smoke.
                    —Rebecca Harding Davis

She wrote on gray paper, it seemed, or she caught the smoke in words, spoke an ashen language. She dealt with those who might never have seen the sun, who dwelt in a night of spark-showers, of red-hot pours of rain, a hole whose Heaven was the hell of this one, and there they lived till they fell to the abyss of that. *The idiosyncrasy is smoke*, she said, but it was more than smoke: it was tb. too, and maims, and scalds, and the syph, it was souls that never surfaced, it was the death in the dark of moles.

Constance Fenimore Woolson, 1840-1894

HENRY JAMES AND LADY

"Our apartment? . . . . With so many families below us
and only one pair of stairs, it does seem to me dreadfully
public."
"You must look upon the stairway as a street."
                              —Constance Fenimore Woolson

Thus an exchange between two of her characters, but it might well have been she who'd spoken so and he who'd so replied. They'd met in Florence when he was thirty-seven and she forty, and they were friends for fourteen years, but little remains to expand that fact. A few letters, someone else's recollection, and, in a guest-book possibly, once or twice a name—and their fourteen years of knowing end beneath her open window (were the curtains blowing out or in?), in her bones and blood on the paving-stones of Venice.

He took her to the galleries, and to the churches, and they walked, she said, in green Cascine, walked there among the pines and ilex trees, where long ago, he said, Ariel breathed his lines to the Wind, and he may have wreathed them with her hair—*Make me thy lyre,* he may have said, *Be thou me.* Ah, the pictures he must've explained, the statuary, the rituals, the ways of bygone times! As they stroll, their heels tacking down some palace floor, you can see him incline a little toward her, quite the gallant, he, and you can hear his voice, or almost, for he speaks to a particular ear, and his words *seem (you must look upon the stairway as a street)*, and then they're gone, along the corridor or into another room.

Helen Hunt Jackson, 1831-1885

AN EPIGRAPH FOR A SHORT STORY

Q.: Do you want schools on the Wallowa Reservation?
A.: No, we do not want schools on the Wallowa Reservation.
Q.: Why do you not want schools?
A.: They will teach us to have churches.
—Helen Hunt Jackson

Me no Christian!

Horatio Alger, Jr., 1832-1899

NAVIGATOR OF THE WINDWARD PASSAGE

His frank, offhand manner makes him an immense favorite
with the circle to which he now belongs. He says little of his
early history, and it is seldom thought of now.
—Horatio Alger, Jr.

He and his father lie hip and thigh under a dark gray
common stone, but though both were Doctors of Divinity, only
the elder wears a *Rev.* before his name. Near here once, Eliot
preached to the Indians, and hard by too are redskin dead, yet
the apostle is quite forgotten now and his flock a flock of buried
bones. Few stray to this place these days, and fewer know of the
shades, the christian and the christianized, who come calling on
their own. They're unaware, the chance strollers, of the glances
of the gone, they hear no hymning braves, no street-boys' jeers,
they merely pass, the sightseers, and go their unseeing way. If
they stayed longer, would they sense the souls they went among,
would they catch the stalking Amerind and bugger Junior at his
games? How odd, to watch a phantom arrow fly! How queer, a
frockless *Rev.* behind the ghost of Ragged Dick!

William Dean Howells, 1837-1920

THE RED LETTER *A*

When her shame became known to me. . . .
—William Dean Howells

She was a guest of the family, one of the household, almost, and the reason was this, that his mother pitied her, a poor knocked-up seamstress, her plight as yet shown only by her wet, her downthrown eyes. His mother pitied the girl, gave her a seat at table and a place before the fire, loved her, it would seem, and all the more for the fall from grace. Her son, though— twelve at the time!—hated the little stitcher, and he scourged her. *She shall be scourged,* he must've read somewhere, and when her shame became known to him, it was hell he gave her: he was levitical.

He'd've been more seemly if he'd laughed, stared at what her belly held and, for an homeric moment, inextinguishably laughed. A threaded needle, he might've thought, and might've let his little witticism detonate a laugh. Instead, he angered over her sin, as if it were being committed there and then, at the table, before the fire, or lying down with him. Somehow her sin exposed a sin of his, up to now a secret, and when her shame became known, he felt that his own came to light, and he so filled the air with spite that breathing burned her, and she wept. He never spoke to her or heard her speak to him, he never let her know that he knew she was in the room—she was space, she was made to understand, a vacancy, and he pretended, even to himself, that through her he could read the patterns on the papered wall. She wept, the sewing-woman did, but nothing weighed with him—twelve, he was!—nothing swayed his mind.

It troubled him all his life, that stumble at the start, and with the grave in sight—he was eighty years old—he told of the hardness of his heart. He didn't want to die and take the burden with him, the stone he'd borne so long, he didn't want to lie there alone with it, a stone forever wedded to a stone. He sought

99

to be free of it, therefore, thought to slough it with the telling, but he'd've been freer far if he'd laughed at the age of twelve, when laughter was less cruel than rage.

Philander Deming, 1829-1915

A GARLAND FOR THE UNRENOWNED

A careless newspaper paragraph was the sole record of the event. —Philander Deming

The event he wrote of was the death of a character in one of his little Adirondack fictions, wherefore there was no real event, no character, no death, no obituary: almost, it would seem, there was no writer, for what remains of him is barely more than his own imagined paragraph. In some parish register, his place and date of birth are entered, and in some graveyard not too far away—up along Little Trout River, the annals say—he lies under his rum name in stone. *Lover of men*, its meaning, but none there is who now loves him.

Aye, he lies between some dirt road and the Little Trout, near where it joins the Chateaugay. Burke, the village is called, and by few enough, for only two hundred live there, fewer far than those underfoot. They're unaware of the lover of men, they do not care for the dead who cared for them, and therefore this wreath for the *odd one*, as the Burke people thought him, the odd one who wrote in the dim till he died in the dark, who loved to hunt but would not kill—laurel for him, odd one, unsung lover!

100

John Hay, 1838-1905

THE ELEGANT CAPT. FARNHAM*

MAUD: He is rather well off, ain't he?
*SAUL: I rather guess he is, ef you call three, four, five millions
well off.*

In a room of tooled leather, a gilt and cordovan room, the
Captain sits and reads while *objets d'art* await his gaze, the
Barbedienne bronze, the Owari pot, the Limoges or Lambeth
vase. The hand that turns a page bespeaks the man himself,
formed by birth and firmed on the field of blood—the idol of
the Tenth, he'd been, steeled in war at Seven Pines and later on
the Plains. A widower young (and still young), sole heir to
three, four, five millions, the elegant Captain sits and reads. A
caller is announced by Budsey, his cockney fart-catcher.

MAUD: My name is Miss Maud Matchin.

The girl, a shawl across an arm, is well made and shows a
shade of refinement, but to the Captain's metric eye, it is a
garment merely, merely clothes. Her errand here: to gain, with
Farnham's endorsement, the post of Librarian to the city of
Buffland. The Captain, only flesh when all's said, steals a kiss
and stalls.

FARNHAM: I do not know that there is a vacancy in the Library.

The lass, as bold as brass, has a father as meek as tin. Saul
Matchin, his name, a carpenter by trade, a man who knows his
place, a cap-tipper or, if bareheaded, the kind that tips his hair,
and for Maud the height of his desire is the housemaid's bib.
Himself ignorant, he's leery of her flyer at learning.

SAUL: Where do you git all them books?

Matchin has in his hire one Sam Sleeny, a joiner too and a
dumbstruck swain of Maud's. A tear for Sam: he loves in vain.

---

*A synopsis of *The Bread-Winners,* John Hay's anti-labor novel of
1883, with dialogue from the book.

SAM: *I see plain enough. She's too good for me.*

The reader is returned now to the purer air of Algonquin Avenue. From the elegant Captain's threshold, a moment's stroll across the sward brings one to the gothic cottage (three stories of Buffland stone) of the rich relict, Mrs. Jairus Belding, and her daughter Alice, the latter just now home from a New York school. The Captain measures her, even as he has lately measured Maud Matchin.

FARNHAM: *We have to thank Madame de Veaudrey for sending us back a fine young woman.*

At this juncture, the reader is required to dive from that tower of chastity into a sump of peccant humor. Andrew Jackson Offitt, so named by his father "in servile worship of the most injurious personality in American history," is a professional reformer. He is the founder and first treasurer of the Brotherhood of Bread-Winners, a wildcat labor league.

OFFITT: *We are slaves! We are Rooshian scurfs! We are goin' to make war on capital! We are goin' to scare the blood-suckers into terms! We are goin' to get our rights!*

His low brow leaks grease. His mustache is dyed and oiled, and his black hair reeks. His lips are coarse, and when they part, he shows the green piles of his teeth, like those of a pier. The whites of his eyes are yellow shot with red, a pair of fertilized yolks. He fawns and spits with equal ease, and, sly, craven, venomous, and avid, he touches Sam, poor Sam Sleeny, for entrance fees.

OFFITT: *Gentlemen, I have brought you a recruit this evenin' that you will all be glad to welcome to our Brotherhood.*

The gentlemen, viz.: Offitt, who once robbed his own father; Bott, a fake medium; Bowersox, a one-time streetcar driver fired for insolence to passengers and brutality to horses; Foglum, of whom nothing is known beyond his name; and several unnamed sots, botchers, shirks, bummers, loafers, and soapless nobodies. Sam Sleeny, though heartsick over Maud, manages to cough up a question along with his dues.

102

SAM: *What becomes of this money?*

His main characters having now been introduced, the author mines their road with complexity. E.g., Maud Matchin, awakened by his kiss, loves Captain Farnham.

MAUD: *If I am not to be your wife, I must never see you again!*

But Captain Farnham, a skittish kisser, loves Alice Belding.

FARNHAM: *I am shot through the heart by the blind archer!*

And Alice, though she loves Captain Farnham, knows that he has kissed Maud Matchin.

ALICE: *If you renew this subject, I will never speak to you again!*

Among these perils, the tale wends its winding way. Put to the blush by Alice's rejection of him, the Captain goes for a ride in the woods. There, stumbling on a secret meeting of the Brotherhood, he is detained at pistol-point by several roughs, among their number Offitt and Bowersox.

FARNHAM: *Can you tell me what all this means? Are you horse-thieves?*

A VOICE: *We are Labor Reformers! We represent the toiling millions against the grinding monopolies!*

At length, the Captain is released, but not before he has recognized among the Brotherhood the lorn Sam Sleeny, a man no more but a tool bewitched, a hammer driven by the nail of love.

FARNHAM: *(sotto voce): I must see if I cannot get him out of it.*

The Captain returns to his leather-lined life, but not for long is he allowed to nourish in solitude his passion for Alice. A certain Mr. Temple, owner of a rolling-mill ("employer of thousands"), comes to warn him of an impending strike and probable violence.

TEMPLE: *We keep men to loaf with the tramps and sleep in the boozing kens. They brought ugly reports. Some of them concern you.*

If so, the Captain realizes, they also concern the Beldings. He applies, therefore, to the Chief of Police and the Mayor, and when they promise no protection, he takes matters into his own hands by issuing a call to veterans of his old command, the Tenth, and they respond to a man. He then repairs to the shop of one Leopold Grosshammer, a gunsmith and an old friend, and demands arms for his liegemen: two dozen repeating rifles.

GROSSHAMMER: *I don't dink you wants rifles. Revolvers and clubs—like the pleecemen—dat's de dicket.*

Complexity multiplies. Bott, the spiritualist, the table-rapper, loves Maud Matchin.

BOTT: *Miss Maud, I have seen your father and he gives his consent, and you have only to say the word to make us both happy.*

And Offitt, the gadfly—he too loves Maud Matchin.

OFFITT: *I have seen queens and markisses, and I never yet saw such beauty as yours, Miss Maud Matchin, of Buffland.*

But their passion is as nothing in the presence of her own: she has come to hate the elegant Captain Farnham.

MAUD: *He once wanted to be rather too attentive to me, and I did not like it. I would owe a good deal to the man who would give him a beating.*

As the story resumes, it is seen that Mr. Temple ("employer of thousands") has spoken truly. In the workshops of the great city of Buffland, the men down their tools and head for the gates. In the streets, they are harangued by mischief-makers, inflamers, aiders and abettors, and their mood becomes ugly. The Chief of Police goes into hiding. The Mayor goes into a blue funk. In the Tramps' Lodging House, there is free talk that there will be a rush on the rich by nightfall.

A RUFFIAN: *Algonquin Avenue is heaped with riches wrung from the sweat of the poor! Clean out the abodes of blood guiltiness!*

Rallied round the Captain are his comrades of the Tenth, able-bodied all and tested under fire. They have been promised ten dollars each for this night's work, and armed with the pistols and clubs favored by Leopold Grosshammer, they are ready for it. The mob approaches.

A PLUG-UGLY: *An erristocrat hung to every lamp-post!*

Led by Bowersox, who carries a slung shot, the rioters flood the Farnham lawn. The Captain orders his men to repel the invasion.

FARNHAM: *Forward! Guide right! Double time! March!*

A melee ensues. The Captain clubs Bowersox, but in so doing he slips and falls. Bowersox is about to brain him when he is shot by Mr. Temple ("employer of thousands"). After a hot fight, the invaders are turned back, and the first concern of the Captain, of course, is the condition of his men.

FARNHAM: *Is anybody hurt?*

A fellow comes forward, his face bloody.

FELLOW: *I've got a little bark knocked off.*

There is no time for more, for word now comes that Offitt and his lowlives are seeking a softer touch than Farnham and the Tenth.

LOWLIFE: *Jairus Belding's widder lives just a step off! Lots of silver and things!*

In a violent assault, the hooligans carry the Belding house, and the widow and Alice are taken with it.

OFFITT: *In the name of the Revolutionary Committee, we have called to collect an assessment!*

To obtain money for them (as they think), Alice goes upstairs. Although guarded by Bott, she cleverly eludes him, and rushing to a window, she cries out to Farnham in the night.

ALICE: *Arthur!*

With her instinctive use of his Christian name, her face mantles, and she prays that he has not heard. But he has heard, and at the head of his veteran band (Seven Pines! the Plains!), he comes to the Beldings' rescue. Reaching the upper floor, he corners Bott and pitches him from the very window through which Alice had called that *caro nome*.

FARNHAM: *Look out below there!*

The Captain taps on a door that Alice has closed on herself and her rosy confusion.

FARNHAM: *Miss Belding . . . ?*

Alice opens the door, still crimson.

ALICE: *Good evening, Captain Farnham.*

By this time, the Tenth has routed the foe, and Mr. Temple ("employer of thousands") suggests that it would be wise to disperse the loitering rabble. The Captain agrees.

FARNHAM: *Company, attention! Right, forward! Fours right! Double time! March!*

Of the malcontents, only poor Sam Sleeny stands his ground, brandishing a hammer. Using his club, the Captain fells him with a blow to the head.

FARNHAM: *I think I have seen this man somewhere.*

With the strike up the spout, Offitt turns his talents to winning Maud. He borrows Sam Sleeny's hammer, initials it SS, assaults and robs the Captain, and leaves him for dead, first placing the weapon where it is certain to be found. Then he goes to the authorities and peaches on Sam.

OFFITT: *The most painful act of my life.*

Sleeny is arrested, but he escapes and makes his way to the Matchin house, where Offitt is trying to persuade Maud to elope with him to Paris. Sleeny hurls the miscreant to the floor, places a knee on his chest, and breaks his neck, thereby killing him.

MAUD: *Oh, Sam! Don't leave me alone! Stay till father comes!*

106

Sam stays and is arrested again. When tried, however, he is acquitted by the jury on the ground of temporary emotional insanity.

FOREMAN: In our opinion, there is no probability that the malady will ever return.

Under Alice's sanative hand, the Captain's convalescence is rapid, but still believing his attentions unwelcome, he books passage on an early steamer for Japan.

FARNHAM: (aside): I am inferior to her. It will be only civil to announce my departure.

But when he goes to bid her farewell, she sings him a song.

ALICE: "Could you come back to me, Douglas, Douglas,/ In the old likeness that I knew,/ I would be so faithful, so tender, Douglas,/ Douglas, Douglas, tender and true. . . ."/

It may be imagined whether the elegant Captain Farnham ever sailed for Japan.

The fate of Foglum is not revealed.

Sidney Lanier, 1842-1881

A MOUTHFUL OF BLOOD

Pretty much the whole of life has been merely not dying.
—Sidney Lanier

Five or six was all he could've been the first time he blew an air reed against the column of air in a flute. Thereafter, though words were what he wrote, somehow they seemed to speak as notes, flights of trills and triplets such as birds might've made, and you thought you heard the warble and murmur of a bird's syrinx. His writing pulsed with brilliants of sound (*I send you,* he said once, *a little poem which sang itself through me*), it was spangled with bright and vibrant shivareens. Lyrics rose in him, filled his throat, and flew away. Often too they filled it to bursting, wherefore one day it would not be wrong to say song killed him.

107

Walt Whitman, 1819-1892

A HELL ON WHEELS

*The long brown path before me leading wherever I
choose. . . .* —Walt Whitman: *Song of the Open Road*

To him, this must've been a flat world, where roads ran
without end and always away from a place called here. There
must've been no rim around it beyond which nothing, there
must've been more than seven wonders for him, more than four
winds, more than a three-in-one God and a solitary sun. He was
hardly in his grave when they that trust in chariots began to pave
it, along with his winds and wonders, his triune Gods and suns.

Did he dream down there of the last tree to go, the last seed of
the last stand of grass? Did he hear the last gasp of the last mouse
or mole, did he see the last house fall, the last hole fill, and the
long brown path, did he know it was six feet down, with him?

Ambrose Bierce, 1842-1913(?)

AN OCCURRENCE
AT THE STYX RIVER FERRY

*I love the dead and their companionship is infinitely
agreeable.*

—Ambrose Bierce

It was his asthma, we're told, that kept him on the gad, a
livelong search for disembarrassed air. He'd quickly arrive and
as quickly leave, as if the asylum he pursued had shut its doors
and moved away. That's all he was up to, seeking a sanatorium
to ease his spasms and quell his râle—that's what drew and drove
him, they say, a place to free his bated breath. But they mistook
the man: the goal of his long-drawn chase was death, and he

dogged it all his life.

He coursed it as though it were a species of game, studied its terrain, its ways and hours, its own particular prey, became a mine of old campaigns, till, a soldier rising twenty, he himself began to kill. In the Rebellion, he was cited fifteen times for the red badge he was thought to wear, and he rose in rank from meat to major—but it was only death that he sought, the bright and brass-buttoned Angel. He failed to find it at Corinth and Shiloh, failed again at Stone River, failed once more at Kenesaw, though there, with a Minié ball in his head, it came close to finding him.

The warning was writing on the wrong wall: he was still fighting when the war ended, and thereafter he fought with his quill through fifty years of peace. Into his printed stint, he wrote a duel a day for the papers and on a good day more, and he wore a pistol for the beasts he hated most, vicious dogs and men. He frequented graveyards, walked among the stones and tombs, read the names of buried bones, but always death had been there before him, delivered its dead and gone—and then his son was killed in gunplay, and from there to the end, dirty cerements filled the doré skies.

He came at last to the river. The Rio Grande, it was called, but its name might've been the Chickamauga, which in Indian meant *River of Death*, it might've been the Acheron or known merely as the Black Water, so rank, no mephitic, that no cup, no can would hold it. Whichever it was, he reached its bank one day, and there, not far from the crossing. . . .

Henry James, 1843-1916

A *CONVERSAZIONE* AT HENRY'S

"It's why one came out," Strether went on. "And it's why one has stayed so long. And it's also"—he abounded—"why one's going home. It's why, it's why—"

"It's why everything!" she concurred.

—Henry James

His guests dwelt in some element of their own, less than water and more than air, a mist, it might've been, a gas that slowed the pulse and softened sound, and in it life idled, like steam in a bath. They spoke in parts of speech, rarely with a predicate, as if all their verbs were intransitive—a sort of exhalation, their talk was, a sighing in words, birds of thought too weak to walk or fly. It was a place where language wasn't quite *used*, at any rate not in the sense that money spent was gone; rather it was *tried*, tried *on*, even, like a hat, a boot, a set of furs, and therefore nothing said seemed final.

Beyond the walls lay that which they knew as *out there*, a surround where calls might be made, but only by patrons (no card, of course) to bid on a *pièce de virtu* or to endure some secret service on the hair. For the rest, it was a hell of appetites, of new and impingent horrors. Within was the better world, the one where the desires, the horrors, were all in the past, and of these those who'd been invited there drifted about and spoke. It was high-class gas, with tone colors and clang tints, with innuendoes, half-questions, hints and hinted replies, with leads and lures, their hooks hidden as in feathered flies, with italic glints among the roman lines. Ah, what delicacies they achieved, what pinnacles of meaning they built!—all in denial of *all that* outside.

Emma Lazarus, 1849-1887

PERSONS THAT PASS

. . . shadows that remain. —Emma Lazarus: *Journal*

Somewhere, in some Aryan history of the Jew, she came upon the old apersion, that it was they who'd wrought the Black Death on true believers, who'd poisoned the wells and air, cast the spells, killed with incantations and the power of their eye—it was all the fault of the fall-guy Jews. For this, they were

110

denied their lives, and when sent to the stake for their own black death, they cried out for a pyre with a floor above the fire, that they might do as Miriam did with her timbrel—dance—and, the boon granted, to some Jew tune they died.

Persons that pass, she wrote.

Henry Demarest Lloyd, 1849-1903

ABOUT JOHN D. (BAPTIST)

If the people know, they will care.
— Henry Demarest Lloyd

To let them know and make them care, he sat himself down and wrote a book for their benefit. Five and a half years it took him to tell the story of John D.'s oil, and then the people knew, he thought, and he waited for them to care. He was still waiting when he died, in another century, and he's waiting yet, in another world. On the last page, he'd said *Democracy is not a lie,* the very point he'd had in mind on the first, five hundred and fifty pages away, but it *was* a lie, and the people proved it: they knew and did not care.

In that tome of his, he never once used the name John D.—like the Tetragrammaton, it was incommunicable—but all the same he meant that soiled purifier, that washer of feet with dirty hands. He told how the sordes had come there, crude pete, it was, and the copperas of bookkeeper's ink, and it was dried blood, and wet blood too, it was the smirch of jingled chink. Nothing did he give, the pallid Christer, and much did he acquire, whatever lay in sight, certainly, lands, iron roads, rights-of-way, pennies, facts in whole, and facts in fraction, and he made his as well what could not be seen, the iridescent juices of the earth.

The book told of such takings of his, and it told too of his taking ways. It told of frauds and conspiracies, of bribery and

111

adulteration, of threats made and threats made good, of dynamite and mass murder in burning oil, it told of pinchgut piety and metastatic corruption—it told, above all, of eight-armed greed, of octopodon John and his need to devour man. He was like unto the beast of Revelation risen up from the sea, and with his power over all kindreds, over all tongues and nations, who was able to make war with him?

Not the people! The people worshipped the very mouth that dribbled their lymph and rheum. They knew and did not care.

Henry George, 1839-1897

I AM FOR MEN

There are no classes.   —Henry George

He was wrong about that, and the longer he lived the better he knew it. He came from the poor—in a good year, his father made two dollars a day—and with the poor he stayed. It was pinch at the start and grind all the way, and never the strait widened (he begged once from a man in the street), never the stringent eased. A lifetime in hock, and he ended on a dole (some of which he gave away!), and he lies now in a Greenwood hole, a minus under a plus-sign cross. *I am for men,* he'd said, and by the numbers, he died owing them.

How few were aware that they owed him! Owed for what—that craze of his? that *niaiserie* about the land belonging to all, as the air did, and the sea and sun? It was frivolry (what else?) when he held that none could own the earth in fee, none sell it to another or bequeath it away. *I am for men,* he'd said, but when he failed to name the ones he meant, they knew he was against. The rich knew it, because they always know their enemies, and the poor knew it that never know their friends. *I am for men,* he said, meaning men in common, camaradoes hand in hand, but when he spoke of land, each hand became a fist, the rich that once were poor, the poor that would be rich. *He* owed, but no one owed *him*.

112

Sarah Orne Jewett, 1849-1909
Winslow Homer, 1836-1910

THE STATE OF MAINE

I paint it exactly as it appears.   —Winslow Homer

It is change that is so hard to bear. —Sarah Orne Jewett

They lived and died a carriage-ride apart. It was only a day's
journey from Prout's Neck to the Piscataqua, forty miles direct,
fifty along the shore, but either way, among the rocks or
through the firs, it would've been a hard Maine road before she
came to his place or ever he came to hers. So the chances are,
they didn't try the forty miles of woods or the fifty stone, and it
may well be that neither had known the other's name. And yet,
they seem to have met, those two, that twain, they seem to go
hand in hand, those locket halves of one. More than their
Maine was going, more than that point of land he painted, more
than the pointed trees she wrote; all was going, but for their own
going moment, they held it a moment back.

Lafcadio Hearn, 1850-1904

ON RAISING THE COAST OF JAPAN

I want to die here.   —Lafcadio Hearn

He saw it first from a ship's deck at dawn. The light, what
little there was, flew low, skimming the sea like a flight of
petrels, and it tinted the water, pearled the mist, glinted on a
cone of snow that seemed to float free of the world, a shape more
than a substance, a mountain made of cloud. He must've been
spelled with wonder when he saw it, he must've held his breath
till the bond unbound him. *I want to die here,* he said, and he
was nearly dead then with ravishment.

113

He had hated steam, disorder, kerosene, fled them all his life, dreamed of a Wave that prayed to remain a wave forever, only to hear the Sea say *Nay* and bid it break. And now he was far from the stone and iron rage, the frenzy for size, speed, the freedom to take more than one's need. This was the Garden given again, Eden as found, not as made, and in bliss and adoration, he longed to kiss the ground. *I want to die here,* he said.

And one day, fourteen years later, he did die there, and, dead, he was buried there, but by then the disease he thought he'd left behind (the Wave now prayed to break) had spread to where he lay.

Mary Baker Eddy, 1821-1910

FAITH IN THINGS UNSEEN

All is God, hence All is Good. —Mary Baker Eddy

It was hard to tell whether her sentences were coming or going—they read equally well from the front and ass-end-to—but despite what she wrote about God, He wasn't quite as all-good as she claimed: the first half of her ninety-year life was an all-bad dream. Born frail, she wasn't expected to have a second half, not with those fits she had, those spells when she fell to the floor, screaming through a sponge of spit and voiding in her drawers. Sound was pain to her, or so she said, and they had to deaden the road that ran past her room, and there was something wrong with her spine (it was a cross, and she was on it! she contained her own crucifixion!), and almost as late as her wedding-day, she had to be rocked to sleep in a cradle or cribbed in her father's arms. There were seizures when voices cried her name, and she required mesmerists, morphine, a hired man to keep her down—ah, she couldn't live long, poor thing, those throes would undo her, she'd swoon some day and never wake, death would come and take her off.

She was on the small side, all say, meagerly made but with a graceful way of going, and her eyes at times would change size, it seemed, and color, and she wore her hair in spirals around a rouged and powdered face. She struck poses chosen from picture-books (piety, pity, disdain), and though neither bright nor pretty, she used her middling mind and looks to win three husbands and the odd and suety swain: there was always a whiff of lard about her, there was always an Ebenezer, an Asa, a Calvin flipping up her clothes. Still alive at five-and-forty, she'd grown to be a scold, drier, thinner, a chiller of desire, a slow- or no-pay boarder, a guest but seldom and snotty then, high-and-mighty with her host, a slob about the house, and purposely late for meals. A fighty kind of squatter, she was, and one night, the bag and her baggage, she was kicked out in the rain.

What made her live through those dreary, deadbeat, threadbare years, unwell and unwelcome, pinched for the price of staying and the cost of going away? Why go on, when where she knocked, there was no answer? Why with those fits and fears she had, that bad back of hers, that passion she suffered on a hidden cross, why did she stand there outside the door, why did she bear the pain, what did she hope to gain from a future like the present and the past? Who can say, when she herself may not have known?

That was the first half of her life, and it ended as though half was all she'd get. She'd taken a spill (the fall in Lynn, they call it now), and no knife could reach the hurt, no medicine still it, and there was no one to deaden the sound outside or hold her in his arms—she'd never walk again, it was said, never leave her bed except for a colder grave. And then in her strait, there came to her a name, *Phineas, Phineas,* and softly she uttered it, remembering a layer-on of hands in the state of Maine, *Phineas, Phineas,* and she seemed to hear him speak, saying that health was truth and sickness error, that the body was all in the mind, and the mind through faith could expel what ailed it—*Phineas, Phineas.* Mouth of brass, she knew it meant, and from it she drew another five-and-forty years of life. *Mirabile dictu,* she

115

was healed at last!

Or so she swore—which was enough to give her a start in the paramedical art of curing the rest of the world. If she was as good as her word, she worked many marvels: she made a felon disappear, and a clubfoot unkinked when she touched it with her hand; fevers abated for her, dropsies drained, and a prolapsed uterus returned to place; the halt ran, the deaf heard, and a case of endometritis was unseated by her eye, and consumptions likewise, diphtheric throats,, cancers of the breast and neck, one of the latter so far progressed that the jugular was exposed; she banned the pain of childbirth merely by her presence, and carious bone stopped stinking, and though she lost her own, she grew teeth for others, uppers, lowers, and once a whole new set of thirty-two; and while far from his pillow in Long Branch, she treated Garfield's wound by force of will until magnetic malice killed him. . . .

No more days now of making ends meet, of lacking friends, a home, a spare pair of gloves, a greeting in the street, love, a reason for sleeping and another for waking up. All her needs were filled, or all but one: the immortality she promised her followers she couldn't find herself, and saying *There is no death* to the end, she died at four score and ten. Of the three or more millions she left behind, she gave nothing to the poor: poverty, like sickness, was an error of the mind.

Henry Adams, 1838-1918

THE EDUCATION OF *PTERASPIS*

One must not try to amuse money-lenders.
                                        —Henry Adams

His book wasn't meant for the public any more than he was. A hundred copies were printed, and they went to a hundred friends—a private affair, you might call it, something for the

116

Magi, for the Back Bay blues, and not even all of those, for many made gelt in the three-ball trade, commonly the field of the Jews. But among the best of the best—not the richest, mind you—all along Beacon, the best praised that book of his until not they but death gazed through their ripple-glass eyes at the Common.

There were presidents in his line, his father's father and that one's too, but there'd be no third, and he knew why when he wrote the book: he hadn't grown, he hadn't evolved, he hadn't *become* anything. He was the same ganoid fish that the first Adams came from, cousin to the gar and kin to the shark, but it wasn't enough to have teeth if you had no taste for blood. Blood didn't draw this last Adams, it didn't excite him from afar, feed an appetite, fill a need—in fact, it offended him, as if he lived on thought, on his name, on air, which he didn't, because from somewhere came the cash to pay his bills, some till, some tap he seemed unaware of all his life. Those sail and steam excursions he took, those coaches across the Stelvio, those fairs attended, those seasons here and there—the Nile, the South Seas, Russia, Rome—all those comings and goings that waywore the mind, someone sprang for them, and for his D. C. house and the St. Gaudens figure on the grave of his wife, someone made the tin for him, and someone paid it out.

Maybe that's why he never tried to make State Street laugh. Maybe that's where he got the ready for his tailor and the rent, for the fees and fares, the alms, the tips, the copper trove Kanakas dove for. Maybe he wanted fools to think him wise. The wise never thought him a fool, though. He wrote what the whole hundred would've written had they deemed it worth their while—that a new man had come to rule the world, and that he glowed like that Other One. The differences were small: this one turned wine to water and bread to a stone, and in his creed, a camel would pass through a needle's eye.

Kate Chopin, 1851-1904

A WALK TO THE GULF

I always feel sorry for women who don't like to walk; they
miss so much. —Kate Chopin

She died two days after a stroke had flooded her brain. No
priest stood or knelt at her bedside and spoke of her soul to
Jesus, no oils were felt by her eyes and ears, her hands and feet,
or, seat of her passions, her reins. No oil of olives touched her,
no fatness of oil, and therefore no plea went up for her pain's
easement. She had long since given over wearing the cross that
in her early pictures lies on her breast, but it may have left its
mark, a faint indentation, say, some place that seemed paler
than the rest of her skin. A thin reason, but they buried her in
ground that knew the grace of God. Odd, though, that no trace
of her grave can be found today.

No trace as well of Mme. Pontellier, the self she put on
paper, herself in words, her sentient personation, but quite as
warm as she. Pontellier, she called her fiction, and the name, as
it drifts through the flowered pages, gives off the flowers'
flavor, camomile, pungent and acerb, as if some bitter herb
were being breathed. White, she wears, and it sails her over the
yellow blossoms and down across the beach. She stands near,
watching the Gulf fluctuate like something in the making,
watching its colors flash and fade, and she hears small waves
whisper as they reach for her feet. *They miss so much,* she thinks,
those women who do not walk. They sit, they sleep, secure in
the clothes of stillness, and they never learn the secrets they keep
from themselves; they're poised there, dressed for living, and
living never comes. *They miss so much,* she thinks, and bare for
once in the open air, she delights in the sun and invites the wind.
They miss so much, she thinks, and she wades into the water and
walks away from land.

William Cowper Brann, 1855-1898

THE IDOLS OF TEXAS

*Texas can furnish more bigots than any other section of the
United States.* —William Cowper Brann

The *Iconoclast*, he called that sheet of his, and when he'd
broken one too many images, he was plugged in the back on a
Waco street. He lived about as long as Christ, give or take a bit,
but he made a fight of it before he went: he had a gun of his own,
and he didn't die till he'd shot his shooter dead. Of course, he
didn't rise on the third day; he stayed down.

Booker T. Washington, 1856-1915

"WHAT'S THAT NIGGER DOING
ON THE STAGE?"

*The wisest among my race understand that the agitation of
questions of social equality is the extremest folly.*
—Booker T. Washington

He was making a speech in Atlanta, that's what he was doing,
and one of the things he said was this: *No race that has anything to
contribute to the world is long ostracized.*

And this too he said: *It is important that all privileges be ours,
but it is more important that we be prepared for the exercise of those
privileges.*

And this: *The opportunity to earn a dollar in a factory is worth
more than the opportunity to spend a dollar in an opera house.*

It was at the Cotton States Fair, and thousands were there to
hear him, the whites below the lectern and the blacks in Jim
Crow heaven, and outside stood a morganatic overflow, a hand
at every ear. And when he was done, they rose, those inside, and

roared, they hip-hipped, and they hoo-rawed, and hats were scaled and flowers flung, and fair fine ladies split their gloves while cavaliers split the air. Led by Victor Herbert, Gilmore's famous band played *Dixie*, and the Governor of Georgia, in full view of all, shook black Booker's hand. An ex-slave had spoken to his ex-masters, and his work was found to be good.

Up in the peanut gallery, though, there were those who were not so sure. To them, no old Mose was he and the South no promised land. They thought it a sell, that speech of his, they thought it had the smell of the back porch, the hat in the hand, a yassuh kind of speech, a bow-down speech from a knuckle-down man. A sell, they said, and what he'd sold was the whole black race, and he got no cash for it, or credit either: he still couldn't piss where the white trash did.

What's that nigger doing on the stage? someone said, but who was it? A well-born lady, a horn-player in the band, the Governor of Georgia—or was it simply another nigger?

Woodrow Wilson, 1856-1924

SUMMER WHITE HOUSE, 1916:
two studies

I am above all things else an American.
—Woodrow Wilson

In one of them, eight thousand chairs were arrayed on the grounds of Shadow Lawn, an encampment of camp-chairs, damp as yet from the morning's rain. The verandah too was wet, its railings steaming in the sun, and now and then a stir of air shook showers from the trees, and swaying flowers shone. The people, the crowds, would not be there until later in the day, and the few guards who stood near the gate had nothing to do but wait in the warm noon and watch pennants on the pillars fill and fall, as if breathing the wind.

In the other picture, the chairs were hidden. Not eight, but thirty thousand had come, and at the snapshot moment, they were on their feet and facing the single face to be seen—*I am the candidate of a party*, it might've been saying, *but I am above all things else an American.* Between the camera and the porch, a mass of hats, stiff straws and Panamas, bowls of linen roses, fedoras, caps, and here and there a bared head or no head at all, only the glare off a parasol. *I am above all things else. . . ,* the face might've been saying to faces not in view.

You looked at the man who was looking down, and you tried to imagine what he was seeing, what face he was fixing in crowd, and you wondered back over the years, wondered whether it was you.

Theodore Roosevelt, 1858-1919

THE NATURALIST

I killed two pretty little finches.   —Theodore Roosevelt

He was fourteen when he made the note in his Egypt journal, and he wrote this too, that his shooting was bad, that all he could add to his pretty little finches was a bulbul and a warbler. His style stayed the same for the rest of his life—he was always killing something, always admiring it after it was dead. At fifty, he was drawn again to Africa, this time with weapons to stand off finch attacks: a Springfield 30-calibre, a Winchester 405, and a double-barrelled 500-450 Holland. His coonskin hat from the Badlands was hardly suitable for the bush, though, so he took his Cuban felt along and a helmet made of cork. There were Swahilis, of course, for the guns and grunt-work.

God knows how many finches fell as pellets sped toward other game, the francolins and spurfowl that died of lead meant for the kudus and the reedbucks. On the Kapiti plain, the Kikuyus heard a great crashing all through that year, and it was heard too in the Rift, and among the Nyanza reeds, and in Jubaland it was heard beside the running streams—yea, a great crashing came from the yews and aloes and euphorbias, for game was falling in all those places, oryxes, klipspringers, elands, rhinos, giraffes, oribis, gazelles, the last of these graced with lyrelike horns, an embrace, they seemed to be. And gerenuks tumbled in the brush and grass, and topis, and nine lions, and duikers, and dikdiks, which are antelopes no bigger than hares, and birds were blown to feather snow, bustards, cranes, marabous, geese, grouse. . . . Aye, a great crashing was heard in that land!

I killed two pretty little finches, he wrote in his boyhood book, and the boy at fifty noted this: *I shot a white pelican with the Springfield rifle; there was a beautiful rosy flush on the breast.*

Alfred Thayer Mahan, 1840-1914

THE FLAG FOLLOWS TRADE

As regards the problem, take the islands first and solve afterward. —Mahan: *letter to Theodore Roosevelt*

He was saying nothing original, really. Reduced to its l.c.d., it was the same old thing—that if you wanted your share of the world, you needed a navy to reach it and a navy to bring it back. There was nothing new about that. It was stale before steam, known before sail; it was *abc* to ancients who went out on the currents and came home on the tides. It wasn't green even when seen on the page: there too it was long in the tooth, young only in a bygone age. He seemed, moreover, to write down his nose, as a better-born Christ or a gentile Moses, and he used a language as unwieldy as snot, a stringy sort of lingo—papal, almost—that jigged and grew and broke. All the same, it got him quite a few free suppers and a dozen or more degrees.

It was no surprise to anyone that he took the scriptural tone. He'd been evangeline even as a cadet. A snitch, they thought him when he put a classmate on report, and thereafter, bate the odd prig, they cut him to a man. Nor was he liked any better when he trod the deck: as he rose in' rank, he sank in favor, and to fellow salts, his flavor was nil.

Not so abroad, though, and not so here to Teddy R. To such, that sea-power book* was the last one in their Bible, the real Revelation, an epiphany, and where the Captain went, he left a phosphorescent wake. It led to those islands, and on later maps, each took on the color of the main. Their people, of course, did not change. They were what they'd been before: niggers.

Owen Wister, 1860-1938

EVIL HAS NO FIRST NAME, GOOD HAS NO LAST

Lounging there at ease against the wall was a slim young giant, more beautiful than pictures.
(Jeff, in *The Virginian*)
There was in his countenance the same ugliness that his words conveyed. —(Trampas, in *The Virginian*)
—Owen Wister

One shines forth all virtue, the other sums up all vice. Each, having begun with a single untinctured quality, retains it to the end, each remains absolute, pure even in impurity. They vie on several occasions, these opposites, four, perhaps, or five; over language once (*When you call me that, etc.*), over matters of will and ways of life, over stray souls, and finally over who shall kill to stay alive.

A parable for the new nation, a fiction clothing a fact, and thin enough the disguise: how can the sinful enemy win, how can we lose that do no wrong?

The Influence of Sea Power upon History

123

Hamlin Garland, 1860-1940

A FLAT ON 105th ST.

When "The Black Riders" came out, I was touched to find it
dedicated to me.   —Hamlin Garland

His place was up along Manhattan Avenue somewhere, on
the morningside of a ridge, and over a hollow square of roofs,
he could see the Block House in Central Park. Clotheslines
intervened, and there were chimney pots that spun in the wind,
and phone-poles leaned as the crosses did on Calvary, but
beyond all such, trussed by rope and wire, rose the remainder of
four walls, the reminder of a war fought just around the corner
and a hundred years away. He may have stood there, staring
down at history, or, since he had a caller that day, he may have
put it at his back.

The caller was two-and-twenty at the time, and in eight more
years he was due to die far from that uptown flat and further still
from where he'd lie. In the town of Badenweiler, he'd some day
drown in a pleural effusion, and they'd bring him home who'd
never known one. But meanwhile, not yet dead, he sat in a worn
gray ulster doing as bidden by his host, writing the five poems
lined up (as he said) behind his eyes, arrayed in a rank in his
head:

Once there came a man
Who said:
"Range me all the men of the world in rows. . . ."

And the host marvelled that such a thing should simply come
into being, reach life whole, and he felt as though he'd
witnessed a birth.

His road would be longer, but there'd be less to see on the
way: in all his eighty years, he'd pass no black riders ranged in a
row. If he knew that then, he may not have watched his caller
write himself dry. He may have turned to the window and
gazed at some ruins that stood on a hill.

Stephen Crane, 1871-1900

HIS NAME WAS HEART'S PAIN*

None of them knew the color of the sky.
—Stephen Crane

He liked the waifs and strays of the world, the loose leaves.
He liked foundling cats and dogs, on-the-towns, boes with
burlap underwear and newsprint in their shoes. He liked the
hand-to-mouth kind, those with nothing for the dry or rainy
day, the ones they fished from the river or found in a drain,
snowbirds, paregoric drunks, hatcheries for the spirochete. He
liked the skim, the slough, the eyesore, the round-the-corner
queer. They were the last of the free.

He too traveled light, as if he knew the way would not be
long. He took his Cora, the whorehouse madam, he took his
bad teeth, his tubercle bacilli, his six-shooter, and his pack of
mutts, but no maps and no other load than such phrases as
wounds in the rain, and he went from start to finish at high speed.
He died at thirty in the Black Forest, but unlike the clockwise
living, he knew the color of the sky.

Frederick Jackson Turner, 1861-1932

THE FUTURE IS THE PAST

The west looks to the future, the east toward the past.
—Frederick Jackson Turner

By the time he came to Wisconsin, the voyageur was gone
and the Indian going, and there were bee-line slashes through
the pine woods, and roads were growing toward the setting sun.

---

*Title from Poem XLI, *The Black Riders*

125

Across the prairie, tracks flowed as though still molten, and wheels turned where pacs had walked on leaves, on air. The ax was there now, and the plow, and the scythe, and a spew of sons, and then, when all free land had been handed out, the tithe of rent began.

But on the maps, there were white spaces yet, places where rumored rivers ran, where grain grew that none had sown, a main of wheat blown by the wind, and a thousand miles away, some said, a snowy range, a wave, seemed about to crest and break. And they went there, the sons, the dispossessed, they streamed westward with the grass, rolled the frontier back some more, to the sea this time, to where the sea set sail for Japan. Ishmaels, they were, and they'd reached land's end landless, and the hands of all were against them, and theirs were raised against all. . . .

> They put sixteen men on Cape Cod beach,
> And on their shins they were heard to say
> "Jesus" to start with and "Jesus" ending,
> Their word, or so the redskins thought,
> For what the bowdowns sought in the sand,
> A bead, it might've been, a shell, a strand
> Of weed, something lost that must be found,
> And the savages said, "Who or what is Jesus?"
> And they were told "The Power of the world."
> "Your search is over, then," the savages said,
> "For what you seek you hold in your hand."
> "But we see only sand," the Christers said,
> And then they rose and strode on westward.
> They'd quest to where the day-star drowned,
> And they'd come at last to another beach—
> More sand for the knees, but not there Jesus.

Ah, well, they'd come to steal, and having stolen, they were stolen from in turn, and they'll never know nor ever care that each is his own frontier. The Indian knows—*What you seek, you hold in your hand*—but the white man dies unaware of what lies within reach.

O. Henry, 1862-1910

POOL-SHOOTER IN A BILLIARD ROOM

Turn up the lights. I don't want to go home in the dark.
—O. Henry

In the belle-lettered world, they were always a little embarrassed by him, always put to the blush. He made them feel unmade, as if some private button had come open, undone, as if a trick (*Kick me hard!*) had just been played. He was the inside-out of themselves, basted only and never meant to be shown. It was mortifying, the sort of company he kept, printers, paragraphers, night-court hangers-on, the slumdom of his trade. Nothing was too low for him but respectability: the disquisitor, the scholiast with his stars and superior figures, the splitters of split hair, in short, the pedantry, all that kind he shunned.

He clubbed at quiet saloons, as like as not with train-robbers and even more so with whores. Whores were easy in his company, gave and took, seldom lied to him, loved him for the hour they sold and sometimes, because he never lied to them, right on through to the following day. Such were the things he cared for, and these were those he cared for less, sweatshops, the corrupting of children, hunger, and the rich, and he fled from all strangers, especially if they wrote. He wasn't gent enough for the genteel, sad to say, he wasn't good enough for the great.

127

Arthur Brisbane, 1864-1936

ONE WHOSE FATHER RHAPSODIZED

I was brought up on that stuff.   —Arthur Brisbane

The stuff was Socialism, and it was in the first sound he heard, the food he fed on, and all that stood or moved—the stuff, the stuff, the very nursery air was red or rouged. How early he knew of phalansteries, how soon he spoke of the Four Movements, the Twelve Passions, the grace of work, and the need to appease desire!—he was born in rose, reared on rosy fancy. It nourished the child, that stuff, but, alas, it was not enough for the man; it was fit cheer for the romancer, but it wouldn't assuage a rage to be rich.

A man is what he owns, he'd say one day, and toward that day he made his way with words. Millions, millions of them, a continuum of words, a procession distinguished only by duration and numbers, selfsame ever except for time and place. For fifty years, that stream of language flowed, shallow, flat, without cadence, and not entirely clear, daily that unvarying blot of scrivenry grew, and with it, word by word, he grew too—grew rich. It mattered little to him, not at all, really, that he'd (what was the phrase?) sold his soul. He got paid in gold for it, and when he died, great men in great numbers came to send him on his way.

But to where? To what . . .?

Herbert Croly, 1869-1930

THE PROMISE OF AMERICAN LIFE

The common citizen can become something of a saint and
something of a hero. —Herbert Croly

His book all the same was addressed to the few. An encyclical
to bishops, it might've been, and it read as if it came from
Rome. The going was an everglade of language, spongy,
sawgrassed, and dense enough to dim the way, detain and stay
the plain and simple mind. The exceptionals, though, had little
trouble with it. In truth, they rather approved the soft, the sunk
and sinking prose, and thought them all to the good, those
serrate pages: they were bare meaning and meant for the rare
kind of eye. What the book called for was the keeping of the
Promise.

From our knees on its eastern strand, it seemed this land
would never end: there was no west; there was only westing.
Endless too the fruits it yielded, and, our praying done, we
were free to rise and run toward riches. They were there in
evergreen plenty, and we all of us ran, crying *Mine!* as we went,
Mine! through a pair of handsome centuries. But there *was* an
end, and one day we'd reach it—on another beach, we'd find the
sand we began with, and there'd be nothing ahead but Japan,
nothing behind but what we'd had and lost.

And now the pastoral letter came, involuted, a sidle of words
like a crawl of crabs, and it called as it came on the few. They
were told as before of the woe in store for the full—the full shall
hunger, they heard, even as they did in the Sermon on the
Plain, nor were they to laugh, for pain would make them
mourn and weep. They were to keep the Promise: they were to
disown because they owned, lose because they'd won, they were
to give not for gain but the good of many: the Promise must be
kept. And when they understood, those kings of all, they
mourned indeed and wept.

After a few wars and revolutions, the book was forgotten.

Gustavus Myers, 1872-1942

THE GREAT AMERICAN FORTUNES

A virtuous and superior order ought to produce virtuous and
superior men. —Gustavus Myers

There are no books about him, only a strew of facts in nooks
and corners, a broken string of beads. They've rolled, the few
known wheres and whens, and, strung anew, they make a
shorter strand, as though not all the lost were found. He was
born somewhere, and somewhere else he died, and on neither
place does a plaque appear, nor does his face grow worn on a
coin or his bronze stand poised in a park. He simply came,
wrote for forty years, and simply went away.

It's almost as if he hadn't been: he hardly made a dent. What
he wrote about, what he spent his life on, was the theft of three
million square miles of earth, the transcontinental haul. From
start to finish, that's all he meant to tell of, how the open road
had closed. Aye, Cameradoes, great Companions, how the open
road had closed! We trespass now, we pioneers, but, strangely,
we have no hatred for the order: we merely hate ourselves for
being poorer than the rich.

Benjamin N. Cardozo, 1870-1938

HEAR, O ISRAEL. . . !

In the cathedral of the law . . . spire and minaret and dome
still struggle toward the skies. —Benjamin N. Cardozo

His father was a thief. A pocket Judge, he'd been, and the
pocket none but Tweed's, an unclean place to be, he a sephardic
Jew, a spanish-portugee, and he was all the more impure for the
skullcap he wore, the laws of meat and milk observed, the

130

forequarters eaten, the unleavened bread, the bitter herbs: he was a *pious* thief. Writer of writs and fiats for a fee, false scribe, Star-of-David renegade, high one of Israel come low—*Shema, Yisroel*, hear now of the son!

He was stainless, those who knew him say, a seraph with wings for foot and face and a twain with which to fly. He chose to remain on the ground, stay where his father had thrown himself away, walk when he might've flown. It was as though no life were possible but the one he resurrected from the mire. He felt bound, it would seem, to redeem his father's time, and therefore what flights he took were of the mind. He wrote in passages like those of birds, feathered glints, flocks that wheeled overhead, turned tail, tumbled, dove, and whirled again, gray and rose, his words, pearled—but he, redemptive son, spent his life on the earth, with a sister but not a wife, as if he'd meant from the beginning that his blood should end with him. It did, but in the cathedral of the law, he built himself into a wall that would be among the last to fall. Hear, O Israel!

Frank Norris, 1870-1902

FAR ABOVE OUR POOR POWER

Life is not always true to life.   —Frank Norris

There would've been, if he hadn't died, a trilogy on Gettysburg, a volume apiece for those three July days when blues and grays collided in peach orchards and wheatfields and among the stones in a graveyard. There would've been another million words about high-water marks and bloody angles, about Spangler's woods and the Spangler spring that both sides drank from, another million words about the small wonders of war (the tintype that would stop a ball, the Bible that would not), about shame and valor, about death that came in numerous ways but never twice the same.

131

He'd tried his hand at painting once, in Paris at the Julien. He planned a canvas of Crécy, wall-wide, it was to be, with mercenaries from Genoa, feudal levies, and the crested knights of France, and there'd be flights of English arrows, iron currents in the ocean of the air, and the slain would tint the hills with heraldry. Clearly in his mind he saw the sixteen charges made by the French, and clearly too sixteen retreats, clearly the hues of those sixteen tides and, as the day wore on, the way they changed—but, more's the pity, nothing coursed his arm, nothing flowed from his brush, wherefore all those archers went unvarnished, all those lackluster serfs merely fell.

With Gettysburg, though, words would be his paint, not for the width of an atelier, but for the miles that ringed the Round Tops, the creeks and roads, the groves, the old headstones on a ridge. There'd be pages of sound, color, motion, smoke, malodor, and disorder, there'd be masses resting, marching, running toward death and running away, there'd be shot horses, fallen and falling men, guns bursting, broken trees, sabres, wheels, drummer-boys, there'd be stainless flags and flags like flown bandages, and there'd be splashes of blood on peaches and wheat, blood in the springs and runs, blood in dots and dashes on the rocks.

He'd have to get up the subject, of course, pore over the histories, the orders, the reports, haunt the arsenals and military museums, but having done all that for Crécy, he could do the like for Gettysburg. He'd forget about coifs and hauberks and genouillères, clear his mind of the Black Prince and the blind King, the squalls of arrows that hied through the air, the queer silence of archaic war. He'd fill himself instead with the names of brigadiers and the numbers of the missing, with oddities and ironies, with heart-rend and happen-so, and he'd know where the 9th of Georgia broke and where Sickles lost his leg. He'd paint that lore in words, a million, it'd take, and some, where he dealt with carnage, he might even print in red. . . .

He was nearly gone when he first mentioned the work, only weeks away from being killed by a blown-out appendix, but what if he'd had more time, spilled his million words, said his bookfed say? Would he have said it better than the tall man had done, the tall sad worn luminous man who'd spoken for two minutes after the two hours taken by the speaker of the day? Would those million words have ravelled out the war at last—or had the tall man long since made it plain, from the back of an envelope, why so many thousands had fought each other dead on those fields, and up and down those mounds, and along those one-way roads?

Vernon L. Parrington, 1871-1929

A SWORD TO FIGHT WITH

Centralization is shaping its inevitable tyrannies to bind us.
—Vernon L. Parrington

Aside from a few facts in a bluebook, the loose-leaf pages of his life have largely blown away, and what we know now is where and when he was born and when and where he died, the schools he attended, the degrees he held, and a name or two, a place, an oddity like his hands, to tie him to the world. That we're sure of, his love of dinting loam, shoving those blunt fingers deep to churn it for the peony, sift it for the rose. Someone noted that for us, wrote it down, and therefore on his knees to flowers is how we feel we see him, saying *please* even for such freely-given things. For the rest, there's merely a faint outline on the space he lived in, as where a picture might've hung, a whiter place on a wall; the sound of his voice is gone, and from the rooms where he taught that populism of his, gone the winnowed air. He's dead, we let ourselves suppose, all but that pair of hands.

We say of him, now that he's in the grave, that the range of his mind was small, that what it sought it found and nothing more, that the ground he thought he'd broken was even then a road, and old. We say we didn't require to be told that man, if

133

let alone, would get and ever get, acquire anything in any number, and that each would tend to end with all. Known, such things, and long before he came, wherefore now we try to slight him, spurning his bite and his bark as well, and turning to other dogs.

We try. But our backs are cold, and they crawl, and we recall those hands of his, and we see them close and open yet, as if they'd outlasted him, and we wonder whether they'll outlast us. Our backs crawl with paresthesia, something seems about to touch us—the poor! the people!—and we the rich seem about to fall.

Jack London, 1876-1916

THE LOCOMOTIVE OF HISTORY

It is the proletarian side of my life that I revere the most and to which I will cling as long as I live.   —Jack London

The crowd that heard him, students in the main, took him at his word and gave him a hip-hip-hooray! and a bully-for-you!: he was on the socialist train, and he meant to stay there. As it turned out, he didn't, not all the way. He had eleven years left to live when he made the speech, it'd take him eleven years to reach for that vial of morphine sulphate, but long before the day he died, he was off the choo-choo and into a ditch.

He liked to let on that he came from the working-class, but if his begetters ever worked, it was only with their wits. His father was a do-nought and a Know-nothing, a crank, a dabbler, quick to marry and prone to flight, litigious, spleeny, a caster of horoscopes, an astrologaster. His mother was bred in money, and what money didn't queer, a fever did: it stunted her growth, and she was half-blind and all bald, given to rages and the springing of fits. She was drawn early to the supernatural, to auras and table-rappings and writings in a trance, and at sixteen such trappings of the spirit fled her from home. To pay for bed and board, she gave piano lessons in a zigzag of towns that began in the Western Reserve and ended in San Francisco, where, in one of those music beds, she came together with the peevish stargazer. The meeting was brief and unlicensed, but it produced a son.

A righter of wrong, the bastard could've been, and he might've made a good one. He was poor enough at the start, God knows, hardly ever seeing a cent of money and never two to clink. He had his hands, though, and they heaved coal for a dollar a day, and a day in his time was long, they swabbed decks and swept saloons, they set pins and delivered ice, and in a jute-mill, they twisted a million miles of twine, they salvaged junk, they slaughtered seals, they steered privateers and defended what they stole, and when he hoboed east in '94, they held him on the rods he rode and rattled the bars of a jail. And then from one of those hands, or maybe it was both, the first of fifty books began to pour! A righter of wrong, he meant to become, an upside-downer, a capsizer of the going order—and by the great horn spoon, he'd be a good one!

The trouble was this, though—he got too used to his barony in the Valley of the Moon, too much an addict of undercooked duck (*Throw 'em through the fire. That's the way—throw 'em through the fire.*), too much the getter and spender to stay on that train. He let a world of starvelings go, all but the one made by those two spook-chasers south of the Slot. He'd never really known the rest, anyway—he'd read about them, drunk and fought with them, weltered in them, bled a river of words in their name, but he'd never known them as human, never quite seen them, never felt they were there except to be kicked some more. In his power-systems, they were *the ruck of races, monkey folk, a wretched muck, dull, maundering, and venomous*; they were *weaklings and feeblings*, they were *whiskey-poisoned slaves, spineless, spunkless, crank-eyed, and misshapen. Cocksure rats*, he called them, *a nightmare spawn, bloated, bloody, skulking, vile*. They did not count, he said, the dark-pigmented breeds.*

Eleven years went by, and then one night all he had left was that vial of morphine sulphate, and while he was going under, he may have thought *I will cling as long as I live. . . .*

---

*These epithets were used by Jack London to describe the crew in THE MUTINY OF THE *ELSINORE*, N. Y., 1913

Theodore Dreiser, 1871-1945

LOOSE FISH FROM INDIANA

Love should act in its heat. —Theodore Dreiser

It ran in his family, that lacing of lust, it was in the cognate blood, a factor from the spindle side: they were a lickerish line—trash, the small towns named their spraddling women and their tumid and teeming men. They had the itch, and top dog or bottom bitch, they took their pleasure then and there, in the courthouse square, it might've been, under a bush or the bandstand, on any floor, in any hall and any pile of fallen leaves. Raff, they were, well-known to granny doctors, drummers, side-entrances, and houses aglare through the night—it was in them all, that venereal yearn, but one got more than his rightful share.

He homed on women, that one, headed for their thighs like a ferry for a slip, women of all ages, all conditions, whores, widows, the wives of friends, lionizers, landladies, servants, cock-smitten schoolgirls, and skirts he grazed in the streets, any ole hidey-hole (sometimes three a day), and when no vagina offered, he made one of his fist. *A chemic flare*, he called his urge, but others called it other things, and none of them was love.

How could he have cared so often, cut himself so many ways, how inside of x could he have honed to be in y? what was there about the next pasture that drew him, what shade of green was the grass? was there better than a best-beloved, and would that better be the last? He wrote much of such matters, of a man and his many women, dwelt on his transient fancy, his way-station stops, his arrivals and departures in the dark: somewhere before the end of track, he thought, he'd reach Perfection! He never wondered whether all unknowing he'd already passed it by. For him, the pink was always further, wherefore at death he must've kept on going.

Dead now, he quests in the celestial with his one good eye and his eternal erection. From soul to soul, he goes through the sweet by-and-by, never looking back for what he might've left behind him. Could it not be there, that Ideal, could it not lie in life among the tea leaves that tea-readers read for him, among the pins he retrieved, the whole and broken horseshoes he believed in, the little Jews who brought him luck? could it not be floundering yet in his gluttony and blinded by his flash? would it not be found in the lobbies he haunted, ground between the upper and nether pennies he always pinched? boor, ingrate, liar, thief, would he not turn up the One he sought in the fights he fought over bills, fees, rates, fares, would it not be there still? the common girls he quit for rarer, would not one of those have held all desire, would not, since there was no higher, some millionaire have done the trick . . . ?

An odder stick there never was. He wrote for money only, cash-money, almost, but what he gave for it was people on the page, people like himself, ponderous, fickle, niggardly, and all the time in heat, the women as well as the men. Humans, they were, and oddly enough, for all his seeking, defective to the last, weak of will, fated, rapacious, clothes-crazy, and cursed with clumsy tongues. But somehow, through that swathe of *grammer*, they breathed, they were warm to the touch, they did as he did—to his evergreen credit, they lived before they died.

Robert Frost, 1874-1963

THE PAST IN THE PRESENT

Fearless of ever finding open land,
Or highway where the slow wheel pours
the sand.

—Robert Frost

His poems are chased with roads. They cross on his pages, they wye and unwind, wend among his words for trees, lose themselves in fallen leaves. They seem, though, to lie unstill, to

137

continue, as if each were a rill of time, and as time does, they join where you are with where you came from, they make your life a one-tense thing. Converse, the poems are, people speaking to other people, he, of course, for all of them, and you read less than you listen, you hear the scenes they play in story-teller talk, plain, clear, chosen with care, you eavesdrop on privacies, failings, the tricks of local trades. All this on those flowing roads of speech, and now and then some glowing phrase, a going glint. *The slow wheel pours the sand*, he says, and you see what you'd seen yourself once, you live again through his eyes.

Gertrude Stein, 1874-1946

ALL STIFF AND YET ALL TREMBLING

> *. . . the suggestive movement underneath the rigidness of forced control, all the queer ways the passions have to show themselves. . . .*   —Gertrude Stein

Frying-size she never was, not even the day she saw daylight between her mother's thighs. She came out big and biggened by the year, expanded from goodly to gross and kept on thriving, throve until she died. Clothing always seemed in collapse about her, a down and undulant pavilion, and swathed in its folds were the knolls and dales of her rolling hills, the swales where rills ran and mosses grew, but only God and Alice knew those umber places, knew the mauve secrets of the shade. So enwound, she resembled something snared, a gynecomastic male, beamy, ox-hocked to the point of dropsy, with fat little hands like huffed-up rubber gloves: she did not suggest a she.

In the word, though, she's nothing else: she's the good Anna, and she sees the round around her blind with the-good-Anna mind and eyes. A surprise, it is, to find her women so nearly real and her men so nearly names. You'd've supposed that from such bulk, only the crass and massive would be seen, the occupant things, shadow-makers, shakers of floor and wall, you'd've expected her women to be fur and her men wearing them. Instead, it's a full-breasted world, a world of not-touching men, one where one gender only sways, names the visible, frames the ways—and the other, hardly more than floral, drifts through it like a spore, a lost seed for a lost once-fruitful land. . . . And yet, underneath those clothes, a stir within the stiffness, snows falling in glass balls, swirls alive in amber.

Sherwood Anderson, 1876-1941

THE TRAIN THAT WENT NOWHERE

He had been awake thinking of the journey he was about to take and wondering what he would find at the end.
    —Sherwood Anderson

The westbound left Winesburg at seven forty-five in the morning, and George Willard was on it. His father had carried his bag down the hill to the depot, where several townsmen, a dozen or more, were waiting for him on the platform, and each of them had shaken his hand before he climbed aboard. He took a seat in the smoker and gazed for a moment through the window, but he saw none of the faces that were staring up at him; in their places were those of other occasions, a girl he'd known, a man wheeling a barrow of boards, the town lamplighter, a tall woman in a fine gown. He closed his eyes, the better to dream of old times, to cast and run through old scenes, and when he opened them again, Winesburg had passed from view.

All his life he'd ride that train. There'd be many stops, at stations, junctions, switches, sidings, but always the terminus would lie somewhere ahead, always there'd be more rail: he'd grow old and die on that train, he'd die before he reached his

139

destination. He'd pass different fields, strange trees, unknown people, he'd cross streams wider than the Wine, read new signs, and note new ways, and roads he'd never walk would quickly come and as quickly go. But to what he knew that day, he'd add nothing, nor would more be needed. He held then all he'd ever hold, all he could sort and store away: he had no room to spare for other worlds.

He already knew the spice of the little crooked apples, mulled rain, they tasted like. He'd wandered Trunion Pike at night and wandered the gas-lit town, and he'd heard sounds in the darkness that made it bright with pictures, made his stock of stories repeat themselves, wring his heart another time—*oh, the lovely dear, the dear, the lovely dear!* What awaited him in other places but other loneliness, other dreams without shape, more of the same somber colors and galled lives? All that was deep in his mind now, and he'd find no additions out there, not in any of the miles and years he still had left to go.

Willa Cather, 1876-1947

ON THE ENCHANTED BLUFF

There seems to be no future at all for people of my generation.
—Willa Cather: *diary*

It was still eight years off, the page that bore her particular date, the line she'd leave at some comma, some phrase, at some word she'd just begun or one that remained in her mind—and ahead would lie a ruled void, a future that belonged to someone else. And then it would be said of her that she never had to look for things to see: they seemed to come unsought, drawn by her stillness and unafraid, and they stayed while she wrote of them quietly, keeping her voice mild, her motion slow, and they'd

140

show her their colors as they went about their ways. There was no future, she said, but she put a stop to time, she warmed old suns and made clouds drop anchor, and birds forever applauded on the wing.

Upton Sinclair, 1878-1968

SOCIALISM

Can't you see it?   —Upton Sinclair

They say, if you count his dime novels about West Point, that he wrote a hundred books, and they say as well that no man ever read the lot, and least of all he. They say you can tell the way he fled across a page, and it shows, they say, that he knew where he was headed but never where he'd been. That pell-mell of his to right all wrong—a flight, it seemed to be, a dead run toward where the red sun rose with its daylong morning. *Can't you see it?* he said. *Can't you see it?*

He saw it, and he sought to draw it nearer with his five million words. There was no art in any one of them, none at the end of all—a hundred books, he left, and though they morned the world no earlier (*Can't you see it?*), they told it where to look.

Carl Sandburg, 1878-1967

ALL THE COASTS OF PALESTINE

The prairie years, the war years, were over.
—Carl Sandburg

He was born in Galesburg twenty years after Abe had spoken there in front of Old Main Hall, born breathing air that still seemed dense with the words, a swarm of birds, they might've been, fledged on the prairie, flying its winds, indigenous. From near and far, twenty thousand people had come to hear them, dead now, most of that number, and forgetful the rest, and for such the words had never been said, the birds had never flown. But for this one, born to a pair of emigrant Swedes, the first sound he heard was the drumming of wings, as once it was heard in Galilee.

Abe was long away from there when the Swede first saw where he'd stood, first read the plaque in the wall, fancied feathers falling though nothing living flew: Abe was far south by then, in the Springfield earth, slain and unrisen, bones dressed in a mildewed suit. Still and all, he was here too, as if the space he'd filled was full of his ghost, a ghastly three dimensions. In passing the spot, he'd pause, the Swede, and his mind would turn to another zone, the one that had known the only Son, and he'd see waters wherein two brothers fished and a wedding in want of wine. He'd feel then that he was close to some disclosure, that a light was about to shine on a road about to be known, but half his life would pass before he learned where the other half would go.

There'd be a second Son by the time he was done with a myth that began on a corn-shuck mattress and ended in a bloody bed a thousand miles away. There'd be another Mary betrothed to another Joseph, and the Holy Spirit would find the way once more, to a Bride who lay in Hodgenville. And again there'd be a lost but glowing childhood, as if the sun were behind a cloud, and there'd be growing news of Him, and up and down the land the people would spread His fame, and they'd exalt Him, that

142

King already come, and praise His homely name. There'd be those, though, that hated Him, and He'd die of a leaden bullet instead of iron nails—but He could make a cat laugh, the Swede would say, and the second Christ would rise.

Wallace Stevens, 1879-1955

IN MY ROOM

the world is beyond my understanding. —Wallace Stevens

You'd know him none the better if you reconvened his life, strung the scattered beads of name and number, his place and date of birth, the kind his kindred were, his father's station, his mother's frame of mind. They'd touch again, the beads, but there'd be no fire from such frictions, no light, nor from these, his schools, his friends, the seas he sailed, the letters sent and received, the famines and other murders of his age. Still dim you'd find his page and him, still beads he'd be though stranded on a string. His only gloss is he.

How pervious he seems from here! Between you and him, your room and his, a mere scrim of language, and through that limpid writ, that net, that reticule, you sense the seethe of cerebral motion, an involute of memory, a notion in the making, a skein of prompted nerves—you've been allowed to see a brain. A bright within, lofty, lucid, rare, alfresco, almost, almost of the open air—it's high noon in there, and the sun's *blunt yellow* runs all four walls.

Enter, though, and the light begins to fade. Shadows grow, and then shadows in the shade, the pure, the plain, turns arabesque, a miscegine of meaning churns, nouns are found in shocking company, and colors *(gross blue!)* grossly misbehave. You've come from a teeming terra into one that teems with him, and there's no place inside for what you've brought: your outside words and thought, your extramural you.

In his room, his world is beyond your understanding.

143

William Carlos Williams, 1883-1963

ON REREADING
IN THE AMERICAN GRAIN

'Rather the ice than their way.
—William Carlos Williams

The black cloth cover is a little rubbed at the edges now, chafed down to gray linen, and on the back, the gilt is gone from an ornament and from part of the author's name. It has a used look, as if held by many and fingered much, aged by touch and the tear of time—but for all its show of wear, the book has been read only once. On the flyleaf, your signature in a hand you hardly recognize, curved and coursing, a stream of script striving to be print, and below it a date forty-five years passé. You turn to the title page, where, in the colophon, Pan pipes in silhouette, and you stare at white paper yellowing, milk becoming cream, and you wonder why this pound or so of presswork has followed your goings and comings for all those years of your life: how did it speak the one time it spoke, what did it say that was said for good and all . . . ?

A library, your mother called the place, and you stood before its three stories of red brick and granite, peering through the doorway at walls that were made of books. It was a house of books, your mother had told you, books of every size and color, every shape and kind, some with pictures, some with maps, music, numbers, and all of them with words, and they were kept there for people like you, she'd said, yours to borrow if you promised to bring them back—you could take the walls away! And then, taking you by the hand, she led you through the entrance, out of the small room you occupied and into the world inside.

There was no way for you to store the rummage of reading that stayed in your head: it lay where it fell, on the floor and in all four corners of your mind. There was no constancy, there were no sequences, no series, no fragments suggesting other fragments: there was only a vast and outflung confusion, the lumber wrung by the disaster of learning. The smell of the

144

wilderness was tinged with that of trains, ships went down in serpent seas, cities burned, and tortured blackcoats prayed and died. Wagons forded wheat, and there were onsets and cannonades, skulls, bunting, and explosions, assassins, stampedes, storms of paper and birds, and there were wonders too many to tell, the face of Jesus formed by trees, Sutter's flume, and a box of cheese on a raft, and there were marvels as well in the names, Hocking Valley, Central of Georgia, the Monon, Kearsarge and Monadnock, the Cowpens, the Little Big Horn, and Chickamauga, and biggety blacks hung from heights, black pendulums, and red men ran from village to village, crying *Come! come to see the people from Heaven!*, meaning the whites. . . .

And then into that random, that strew of phrases, tables, dates, and places—a conjunctive for scattered times and disparate faces, a strand for all those teeth and beads and shells of history, a book for books to be written by: *In The American Grain*! You remembered how it had made still things stir for you, how they'd seemed to sort themselves, how they'd begun to fall in line—but forty-five years were gone and with them the key, the why. Would you find it, you wondered, where you'd found it once, would you read what you'd read before? You tried to learn the answer (*Rather the ice*, you thought), you tried, but the pages would not turn.

Sinclair Lewis, 1885-1951

THE MAN WHO WROTE BLANK PROSE

Oh God, no man has ever been so miserable!
—Sinclair Lewis

What with those starveling eyes of his and that pocked and pustuled face, he looked like one of God's ill-used. His hair was a red confusion and his head a skull in skin, nor had the hand of God been cordial to his ways, given him the will or the power to

145

still the din he made with his brays of laughter. It hadn't buffed away his roughness or put him at ease, and he never found a haven here, never felt at home. He was a lout, graceless and loud, and shunned down the road toward death in Rome.

Small wonder, then, that his writing matched him. It heehawed, as he did, it scratched itself, it snotted through its fingers and wiped them on its sleeve. It had an arrhythmic mode of going, uncadenced and accidental, it suffered from the shakes, the fits, it lunged, it strove, and its trail was littered with crumpled phrases and greasy parts of speech—a lifelong strew of language, and not a glitter among the trash. Unseemly scrivener, he offended even with his punctuation.

It took that kind, though, raw, half-smart, and cock-a-hoop, to grasp that his country was the same. No one less coarse could've done it, no one using prose more chaste, no stickler or stuck-up, no man of taste: it took a shitepoke, it took brass to savvy the brazen. They're in his books, the small-town boosters, the Vere de Veres of the barbershop, the pool-hall sloganeers; he's got them pegged there, the joiners, the persecutors, the enemies of the strange; they're in print now, the prim profane, the tellers of salty stories, the spiders in their stores—they're known, and they wear his name.

Ezra Pound, 1885-1972

IN SHORT THE USUAL SUBJECTS

of conversation between intelligent men.
—Ezra Pound: *Canto XI*

They were foreign to us, his queer and cranky ways. We didn't hold with his baiting of the Jews, we said, with his aiding of our enemies and the views he aired on Money; we were aggrieved, we declared, by his averted face, by the cold shoulder he gave his place of birth; it was odious that he dressed

146

as he did (those cape-worn coats, those two-toned shoes), and it wouldn't go down, or wouldn't stay, that he owned little and saved nothing, as though not for him the reckoning, never the rainy day. *Il piccolo trovatore!* Who was he to mock our documents and our sovereign power, abuse our causes, our systems, and our age, and in his railings at the sheenies of Wailing Wall Street, did he not excite domestic Insurrection amongst us, destroy the Lives of our People, ravage our Coasts? The popinjay, the billy-goateed scold—with that lore he set such store by, his dead and dying *linguae*, the trash he talked of metrics, even so what did he betoken but some stiff little chair at Hamilton, say, or maybe at Wabash . . . ?

Lies, all! We know better why we hate him, but it's a lash we enjoy in privacy: he makes us small. The wind of Acts informs him. He has the gift and gabs, reducing us with archival bombast and mint phrases, old and new coin, with cadences and intonations, with slang and chink and jokebook hebe—the rage *loquendi*, he has, and another to match it in ink. The silk scrolls, the vellum-bound libers, the fly- and rat-beshitten screeds of prothonotaries, God knows where he found them, in what vault, what scriptorium, what corner six centuries forgot, and God knows too why he chose to use them, or *re*use, because he seems to have lived before, been himself a bought sword, Ghibelline or Guelph, a *condottiere*, a brawler with the blueballs, a *quattrocento* dicer with the clap. Tongues! he has, his own and those he was given, and in whatever comes to mind, guttersnipe, *provençal*, japonee, in that four-a-day twang *du pays* of his, he rotten-eggs us and, worse, ravishes us with such lyrics as seraphs and birds bandy on the wing. They're pentecostal, those voices he got from the Holy Ghost, and with them he lifts his lays of early times and nowadays, flies his recitations of love and murder, letters, fine steel, and prodigies, *in short the usual subjects*, and in them the wine-sea surges, and the dawn breaks rose, and there are rains, ambuscades, ideograms, and spiteful gods, and doom caroms along blind arcades, *lussurioso incestuoso, assassino, sodomitico. . . .* Dear Jesus, what does he not embrace in words!

Forty years gone from us, he's been, and they've told, the

lines between the eyes, the gray, the skin, and now we bring him home, an old man we mean to try for treason. But if we hang him, we know it won't be for the bees in his bonnet about Money and Jews or for what he said in Rome. It'll be for this—that we fear he'll be remembered, and we'll be merely dead.

Ring Lardner, 1885-1933

WHAT SARAH E. SPOOLDRIPPER KNEW

She knew all there was to know about . . .
—Ring Lardner

He was only one day dead when they burned his body and got rid of his ash, buried it, maybe, or put it on the fitful air. Lost then what Sarah knew, the truths that couldn't be told, a youth's humiliations, were they?, or a shame or two of older age, lost they became in the fire. She knew all once, and now none of it remains: she took care of his wolf.

What a beast it must've been, to stand off sleep till drink or drug beguiled it! What a beast to still him so while dins were raised around him, to fill him so full of hate, and at forty-eight to kill him! Where did he acquire the creature, what dark sight, what night secret joined the two for life, and, God forbid!, did the horror outlive the fire?

Randolph Bourne, 1886-1918

ENCOUNTER ON 8th STREET

The war or American promises: one must choose.
— Randolph Bourne

He walked a good deal, much further than his curved spine would've seemed to allow, and if you'd seen him coming toward you, his cape filled a little by him and a lot by the wind, you might've marveled that he got the distance, those nighttime miles through street and mews. Five feet high was all he stood, and he was as pale as veal, and pinched in, and he had a wounded way of going, like an animal hit and healed, and his head, too large by a size or more, looked to be a spare one he wore when the weather lowered. The singular blue of his eyes, the hands (they say) that blossomed from his arms, such fine things you'd've missed. Instead, you'd've caught the grotesque that his friends were blind to, the galley-west shape, the scarred face, the nearly torn-off ear.

His cape wallowing, he'd've appeared to be something blown along the pavement, a plane figure, a great commotion of goods, and as you passed, a wonder would've stirred in your mind: would you trade him pack for pack, your twist for his twist, your fear for his back? would you swap your lack of bravery for his exemption? to avoid death in your body, would you settle for life in his, misconstructed, stunted, wrung—and safe? And you'd've said *Yes! Yes! Yes, I would!*

It was all a suppose, of course: you never passed him on 8th Street or any other street, never saw or spoke to him, never chose between the war and promises. You imagined, therefore, that *he* wouldn't've made the exchange, that he'd've stayed as he was, physical junk and secure. You didn't dream that he *wanted* to be called, and that when called he'd refuse to serve. He prayed for the chance to choose against killing, but with that jackknifed back of his, he was never asked the question, and in the end, that's what killed him. He died as the war did, far from the front and not reckoned among those lost in battle. He was simply the animal as before, and when somehow hit a second time, the wound had failed to heal.

149

Lincoln Steffens, 1866-1936

THE MUCKRAKER WHO LOOKED UP

The world which I tried so hard to change has changed me.
—Lincoln Steffens

He could look no way but downwards once, down at the straws, the small sticks, down at the dust of the floor: he could not see the Crown that hovered, the proffered nimbus overhead. Long had he been a raker of muck and muck's maker, man, but for all his raking, he knew in the end that he'd only been making a pile, higher ever, ever higher, but always of muck, a muck of mire. Heavy now the rake became, and being old, he grew wiser than before, saw that the sticks, the dust, the straws would always befoul the floor, and that the more he raked away the more there'd be to rake—all man would make it—and he let the rake fall. It was then he found he could raise his head, descry the Crown devolving from the sky. From that moment, though he thought himself celestial, he was merely a part of the pile.

John Reed, 1887-1920

A LAND TO LOVE

It was a desolate land, without trees. You expected minarets.
—John Reed: *Insurgent Mexico*

He saw it for the first time from the roof of an adobe on the Texas side of the river. A mile or so away, across sand, scrub, and a russet stream, it began in the town of Ojinaga. By day, vines of smoke climbed the air, and the sun broke on gun-metal, and pigmy figures crawled, men in white cotton, women in black, and dogs, and when the last light bloodied the sky, toy sentries rode in toward the fires.

A land to love, he called it, and it drew him as the pickets were drawn to warmth. Its colors stunned him like a disembowelment—the yellow water and the tangerine clouds, the red and lilac mountains, the stove-blue membrane all around and overhead. The heat stunned him too: a fanatical sun seemed more to rear than rise, and from ninety-three million miles off, it so enraged the earth that it shook, as if about to explode.

A land to love, it was, and he went there, and in its squares he found strewn straw, and in its streets women wended with water-jars among the droppings of burro, dog, and man. The stink of piss made a new element, thick in the sun and lank in the shade, and saddles stank of sweat top and bottom, and somewhere a game was seen, one that was played with a ball, and somewhere else a nameless grief was sung, and from under vast sombreros, small lives spat at death.

It was a land to love, but the minarets would be in another part of the world, and he would go there too, and die, and lie at last at their feet.

Robinson Jeffers, 1887-1962

UNA

I never dreamed she would die before me.
　　　　　　　　　　　　　　—Robinson Jeffers

In those last days, did the pain lessen? Did her mind clear, and clear her eyes, and from the stone room she lay in, did she see the room outside? Were there mars of cloud on the bay, calms of kelp, levitant gulls and pelicans, did she watch the pellmell sky? Did she try to converse with frequented places, address them by name, say *Bixby Creek* and *Coal Chute Point*, as if they were present, as if they came to return her calls? Did she

151

think of cypresses and topiary winds, did she sun again among the rocks, find an eighth sea in a stranded wave, remember driftwood smoke in the rain? Did pain remit, did she live while dying?

Did she dwell on him in those tag-end days? Did she rerun him on the screen in her mind, speed him past her one last time, years of him in seconds, and did she know, at the edge of knowledge, that her poet had written prose? Did those lines of his march through her mind, that infantry of words, that never-ending foot-parade? And did she, dying, pity him his twelve more years of life?

Marianne Moore, 1887-1972

THE ACCURACY OF THE VERNACULAR!

I scarcely think of any that comes into my so-called poems.
— Marianne Moore

Vernacular, from *verna*, bespeaking (does it not?) a slave born in his master's house, hence, in relation to language (this by extension, of course), native to the people of a particular place, an indigene. Odd, therefore, that you should think yourself free and clear of such ways of speech — and it *is* speech, your poetry, since so much of it seems to enter the ear, to be waves of sound, a master (a mistress) instructing slaves.

In your lines, meanings overlie, like the scales that tile your pangolin — aye, let the pangolin reciprocate, let *it* describe *you*. You're armored too, cap-a-pie, imbricated, involucred with (as you say) "spruce-cone regularity." You overlap yourself, you wrap yourself in bracts of implication, a little of you showing in each, each the tip of something inner, a hinted invitation — come in, it not quite says, through this not quite open door.

Note: lines 45-47 *The Pangolin*

"The giant-pangolin-tail . . . tipped . . . with special skin." There are pangolins with a bare spot under the tip of the tail, used, it is thought, to palp for balance. But the giant pangolin (*Manis gigantea*) is entirely scaled; no skin is visible. Encyclopedia Britannica, 11th edit., vol. xx, p. 677c.

Bartolomeo Vanzetti, 1888-1927

LAST WORDS FOR SCORNING MEN

I now wish to forgive some people for what they are doing to me. —Bartolomeo Vanzetti

What they were doing was this: they were killing him. They were strapping him into a wired chair, they were affixing electrodes to his calf and head, and in a minute, struck by manmade lightning, he'd be dead. *I now wish to forgive some people*, he said, and he forgave them the two thousand volts that would end his life, forgave them the purple foam that would slide down his face while his body turned red and black, forgave them his burned, his desquamated skin, his wide-dilated eyes, his tetanized heart, and the heat retained by his well-done meat. *I now wish to forgive*, he said, and he may have dwelt then on what the Supreme Court had held, that the manner of his dying was not *cruel* as cruel was meant in Article VIII, that it was simply a new tit for the tat of murder, a mere extinguishment. *I now wish*, he said, and even as he forgave the unforgiving, he was dead.

153

Nicola Sacco, 1891-1927

DON'T CRY, DANTE

because many tears have been wasted, as your mother's have
been wasted for seven years, and never did any good.
                                    —Nicola Sacco

He wrote that to his son the day before he died. *Don't cry,*
Dante, he said, and he's fifty years dead now, that wop from
Torremaggiore, edger of shoes, greengrower, lover of weak
people, wildflowers, and *the harmony of the vivid stream*. Fifty
years ago (is it all of fifty years?), he told his son to hold back
tears and love him a little. *Don't cry*, he said, *be happy, but in the*
play of happiness—that's how he put it in that poor English of
his, the edger of 3K(forKelley) Shoes, the tiller of dooryards,
the murderer lost in children, birdsong, dark red roses,
delirian, he was—*in the play of happiness*, he said, *don't use all*
for yourself.

Fifty years this dervish world has whirled, and the wardens
of that Charlestown day are gone, and the electricians, and the
observers for the Commonwealth, and the man or men of the
cloth—all such gone, and in their place now, space. And judge
and jury are gone, and witnesses, and dim Katzmann with his
damp fear of being taken for a Jew, and the Defense Committee
are gone too, and their throwaways are hard to come by, and
what books there were are stored in the stacks. And where all
this while Rosina, whose tears were seven years wasted, and
where Dante, begged by Nick to smile? Was he happy, *did* he
smile? Did he down himself for the weak ones? Did he love his
father as his father loved him?

Don't cry, Dante.

Heywood Broun, 1888-1938

AFTER THE CRUCIFIXION

For eleven years I have not written about Sacco and Vanzetti.
It seemed to me that there was small point in turning back the
page. Now I know that I was wrong.

—Heywood Broun

On the hill outside Jerusalem, who was not silent but the
apostolic few, the still uncalendared saints? Who else knew that
with the crucial spikes the world had changed, that a three-day
stillicide of blood would dye seven seas, dinge the hand that had
merely shaded eyes, the hem merely trailed on Calvary? *Now I
know that I was wrong*, he said, but by then, their Cross a chair,
a pair of wops was eleven years dead. Another agony on another
hill, but, as before, not many knew what they'd seen. Two men,
they thought, two small men had burned in a blue electric fire,
their page had turned, and the time had come for newer things.
They were in the past now and six feet down, one with his stink
of glue and leather and the other of weed and eels, and since no
Son of God had been nailed up to dry, the people, even the best,
had looked away.

But with a blue flame at the base of the back, with purple
foam on the face and neck, and a body cooked red and black, two
small men had died indeed for all. When that became known,
there'd be more blue lightning and more death, a killing of the
killers, and then the air would clear, seem pure again and good
to breathe. Be sure it would, be sure, be sure, but not in eleven
years. . . .

Edna St. V. Millay, 1892-1950

DEAD LETTER
FROM A DEAD LOVER

Life is . . . a flight of uncarpeted stairs.
—Edna St. V. Millay

I wish I could keep you from climbing those stairs. I wish I could make you stand where you are, holding that glass and watching day break through the wine, your mind still filled with the night's reading, still given over to defeat in war, to wandering men, love's despair, and the birth of Rome— vergilian. I'd stop the sun, hold it not quite risen, so that morning, ever coming, never came. I wanted much the same once before—in another war, it was.

We remember, you and I, but you with such particularity that it goes beyond recall. That one day (and one was all)—it seems to replay itself for you, or, better, to run like time unused, and yet you've used it in a new way every day of your life. How many words you've spent on those few hours! how many lines to a passion unpent only once! One conjunction, we had, and you've been fertile ever since, an ovipositing bee.

I felt a less incessant itch. A soldier bearing dispatches, I dealt with martial secrets, the fates of other Troys, wherefore if you thought me hardly aware of your hands (too small for an octave), of you yourself as small (five feet only!), of the red in your hair when lights across the street lit the room—if I struck you as half-alive while you were half-dead, dwell on the phrases you last night read, on arms and Helen and topless towers, and forgive. I did hear the *sunt lacrimae rerum* you expired at the crux, but my mind was on a later war.

It was years before we met again, and though I was still your lover, you by then were my friend. To cover the years, we'd written to each other in print, told all there was to tell of our one and only day, I in my measured way, and you in yours, proclaiming. (In passing, may I say you said *I* too often, personified too much, let the outside world go too far in, rhymed where you might've shaken free of it, might've taken the pins from your hair, and would you not have been well with fewer *ah*s, my dear, and not so many *oh*s?)

But those are things of long ago and gone. What matters now is now, and I want to keep you where you are, holding that wine-glass up forever to a red morning, and never setting foot on the stairs. I wish I could stay you, I wish I knew how to preserve you there—because when you start to climb, you'll die. On the fourth tread, the sixth, the seventh, you'll suffer a throe that'll bar your breath, and you'll set down the glass with care, sit a step below it, and a step below it die. Death, my one-night dear, is also a flight of stairs.

Eugene O'Neill, 1888-1953

SUPERMAN WITH QUALMS

There is always the monotone of the surf on the bar—a background for silence—and you know *that you are alone—so alone that you wouldn't be ashamed to do a good action.*
—Eugene O'Neill at Cape Cod, 1919

He'd swim in any weather, they say, and at any stage of the tide, high, low, or in the rip of change; he'd swim deep water or shoal, water worked up by the wind or stilled by a fall of snow or rain; he'd go in drunk at times, whored-out, recreant, and on certain days suicidal, and he'd head for the horizon though shadows showed on x-rays of his lungs. The sea didn't feaze him: he was a sea of sorts himself, variable and wandering, opposed to all, with black trenches, with monsters seldom seen and never caught. It was odd for such a one to be afraid of lightning, but he thought they were meant for him, those electric accusations (fornicator! bibber! apostate!), and he seemed to shrink when he saw them, as though they'd find him out if he stood up straight.

157

Katherine Anne Porter, 1890(?)-

THE FOOLS FOREGATHER
AT VERA CRUZ

I am a passenger on that ship. —Katherine Anne Porter

From a row of rooftops, the sun pours a salvo of light into the Plaza, white, smokeless, constant, like a snapshot of an execution. It finds its way through the sweet-by-night trees, pinks the blinds of dark arcades. The eyes of buzzards glow, and rounds of brass, and legends pulse on walls, as though the words were spelt in gas—*Pulque puro*, one such throbs, and *No anunciar*.

A few citizens sit in glares of linen, and between their sips of lemonade, they converse in glances, gestures, stillness, stares, speak in all but words. Silently they treat of an Indian asleep on a seat in the shade, of a lame and lurching beggar, of whores that pass in cotton and a higher class in gauze. They laze over limes, these loafers, and in tics and shrugs they phrase, in tappings on a table and clicks against a glass, and they deal, as they range the balconies, with a gray cat, a parrot, a chained monkey, a dog that has the mange.

And then they rise, the linened citizens, and stroll toward the end of life in the middle of a printed page. The waiters survive them for a paragraph or two, cursing gainlessly, as at sweat, when the fools begin to arrive. They too are exudations, the weepage of trains, rooms, cantinas, motor-cars, they seem to seep into view, to flow across the Square. There are Switzers on this drift, and a bride and groom Mex, and there are priests, a pair on tour, and a squarehead Swede is seen, and a strolling-player troupe, and a slew of Dutchmen, one a traveler in canonicals, a merchandising Jew—and, smoke from Havana, the steerage smell of Spics deported, eight hundred and seventy-six in all, ballast for the *Vera* on this crossing of the Styx.

I am a passenger on that ship, she says. I go hand in hand with Mann and Frau, I pet the dog Bebe. I dance with gypsy dancers, I chat with La Condesa, lady déclassée, and that is I, next to the wedded lovers, I nodding to the Jew, I discussing dogma with the priests. I walk the decks with singers, painters, medicos from Cuba, and Glocken the kyphotic freak. I talk to innkeepers, dying healers, officers, I put Bebe through his bag of bulldog tricks. *I am a passenger on that ship*, she says, I'm even in the hold with those excretory Spics. They're headed for hell, she says, and when they sail, I'll sail too. I sidle with the hunchback, beg with the dog, sell birettas with the Dusseldorf Jew. I am they, shopworn, vile, and quick to anger; I am they, gluttonous, lustful, led by the nose like Bebe. *I am a passenger on that ship*.

You one of the fools? Cool coiled lady, quiet, sudden, and serpentine—you one of the fools? Nay, lady, you're merely here to see them off.

Archibald MacLeish, 1892-

PILAR, OUT OF KEY WEST

The mountains over Persia change
—Archibald MacLeish

The fishing was no good that day—there was too much sun or none at all, the breeze was in the wrong quarter, or the water was chilled by cloud, by auguries—and so, as they cruised among the keys, they sat in the glare or shade and drank to many things, and they spoke of friends, of prose and poetry, women, perhaps, and guns, and somewhere in the talk they found a bone to pick. What the row was about, who can tell? One's dead now and the other liege, wherefore they may have fallen out over a great matter or simply a much-ado, a small and instant point such as, say, the way the dead one was shooting terns by the pair, the female on the nest and then her mate in the air. As the *on-dit* goes (who spread the story? who sped it along?), the skipper

159

headed for a nameless reef, stranded his guest, and made for home.

The maroon may not have troubled to watch him go. Standing in a moonstone shallow, he may have looked at a distant rain or at feathers that were lately birds, or he may have lain on the sand, on another Persia, and felt again *the always coming on the always rising of the night*. It was a small earth, that coral isle, merely a pile of limestone spherules (roe, it looked like), but in some creviced pool, he might've seen cities, wars, voyages, disasters, and the future, seen *the trees take leaf by leaf the evening*, seen *the flooding dark*.

He may have heard the turnstones cry, stared at skimmers, sanderlings, shreds of turtle grass, picked up shells and listened to his resonant blood, and he may have wondered when the tide would start to change. Not night then would come to flood the world, but the sea would rise around the key, the key and its yard-high zenith, and rise still more when it was drowned, to his knees and thighs, the buckle of his belt. . . . And then, over the calling plover and the wind, he heard *Pilar's* engines churn.

e. e. cummings, 1894-1963

LUMBERMAN OF THE DISTINCT

you hew form truly   —e. e. cummings

He had a special way of seeing, as if in the rippled mirror of his eye, he saw a rippling real. For him, it failed to hold, the law that controlled the return of light, for him, images weren't simply faced about, right for left and left for right: they were things made of nothing newly, not to be tied to what stood outside the glass. He seemed, with that squint of his, that strophic vision, to get more than one view of the world, to set it askew, to ring and wring it, raze and resurrect it, restore it in a phrase and once in a while a word.

160

A mint language, those lines of his to love and spring, to river horses, whores, and Rome, a language freshly played, sounds made that seem to chime, flicked crystal, falling water, notes of water in the treble clef. And senses mix and trade, transvest attributes, wear unwonted clothes, and nouns, the gist of substance, change. Whores and hippopotami, truly hewn, and so too love and spring, star-old, fire-new.

Jean Toomer, 1894-1967

I AM NOT A NEGRO

One half of my family is definitely white, the other, definitely colored. —Jean Toomer

There was nothing white about that first book of his—it was black almost all, black language, black lyrics on a gray page that would darken in the light, brown with age. It was black-mouth music, and even from the paper, it somehow seemed to sing in black numbers. It was black sound that only a black voice could've made, black verse, and like his twelve-year-old Karintha that youth and man desired, it flashed, a black bird seen in the sawmill smoke, and it flashed. . . .

A whir, he said she was, a blur of beating wings, and she passed as a spindle of dust would pass on the wind. A glinting bird, he called her, and a cotton flower, and dust aspin in the road, and a child with sun-go-down skin that made the young yearn for tomorrow and the old to turn time back. She scorned them, he said, but they worked for her, brought her money, bought her, and she lay with many of them, played *home* with them under the trees. . . .

And then he said *I am not a Negro*, and he wrote himself to death trying to write as if he had no color at all, white, black, or in between. *I am not a Negro*, he said, and with the saying of the

161

words went all the rest of his life. No more books came, caroled or otherwise, only writing that was half-white and half-black, halves that never wholed.

Edmund Wilson, 1895-1972

MOMUS FROM OLD NASSAU

It is unfortunate that there is nobody nowadays to uphold the conservative point of view.   —Edmund Wilson

He was born into a class he called the second-rate rich: there was money around, but it wasn't in sight, wasn't used to light perfectos with, to strew for hounds in a paper chase, to watch on the wind in flight. But the chink was there, and it filled the silver spoon that the little one came with. He was taken on the Grand Tour at twelve, with only second-rate pageantry, of course, and he saw the shrines of Greece and all three spheres of Gaul. Quietly as well a way was found to fund him through the proper prep and proper Princeton, and there were these small spoonfuls too, bespoke clothes, a genteel taste, and ease. His powers, to be sure, didn't come with his keep, but they were tinted by the green all the same.

He was made for the printed word. An element, it might've been, the sea or some reach of air, and he a creature that fed and flourished there, elsewhere dead, the creature fallen or cast upon a beach. He was never much for play or games, but how early he began to read! how vast his range! It was osmotic, his absorption of a page: he had merely to cross it with a glance, and what lore it held was yielded up, was ever after his. He drank in all he saw, it almost seemed, from the *mots* in public places to the scrawl in Aramaic at the feast, and he teemed with dooms and dicta as he policed the world of ink.

There was something of the scold about him, though, the distaff fist, the vixen tone, the rancor in his praise: a rixatrix, he

162

sounded like, sore at faults and more so at perfection. In the presence of written matter, it was as if he were caught in a crowd, elbowed along, compelled, subjected to alien frowst, and somehow stained by nearness, stigmatized. He gave off this, that the right to write was for the rarer kind, not for Does and demos—and yet those were the ones who squidded paper, made known their views, swayed the persuadable mind! From time to time, therefore, he ventured his inventive wing, took a fling at flying, did instead of deemed—he offered a work of his own and became the criticized. The creator survived the creation: the child, alas, died.

So he kept on scolding, holding up the warning finger, shaking it at upstarts, taking them to task. Judgments, he made, and they were decked with allusion and citation, laden with classic names, and here and there, when a thought was expressed in Greek, it glinted like a frat-pin on a vest. He was at it for fifty years. Nobody stopped writing, least of all the unseemly ones, the loud, soupstained, dreary crowd.

F. Scott Fitzgerald, 1896-1940

SEVEN BUCKS FOUND IN A TOILET

All night the saxophones wailed the hopeless comment of the Beale Street Blues *while a hundred pairs of golden and silver slippers shuffled the shining dust.* —F. Scott Fitzgerald

He came out as you went in, and it took your mind a moment to see in the slush downfall of his face the one that once was snow, and by then the door to the hall had stuttered and closed. On the floor near the urinal lay a crush of green paper, two ones and a five: it was his money, you supposed, and picking it up, you wondered how he'd come to drop it where he did. Had he been counting it while he took a leak, reading the print on the Great Seal, staring at the peak of the Pyramid, at God's Eternal

Eye? You looked him up on the directory outside, and with the five and the ones in your hand, you went down the hall to his room. He frowned when you entered, first at you, then at the bills, and then at you again, but afterward you couldn't recall what he'd said or whether he'd spoken at all.

They were about the rich, every page of those books of his, those tales of the age, and he wasn't quite at home there, he didn't seem to belong. He hadn't been invited, you might say, he'd been left out of his own parties, and when he couldn't crash the gate, he hung around in the dark that was made by the light within, somewhere in the shrubbery, behind some tree or car, in the shadows he wrote for the lawn, and if he heard tunes and talk and laughter, it was due to doors he described as open and to sound he allowed outside. He ran after a world he'd built of words, a better one, he fancied, and peopled with the better sort —he honed for it till the day he died.

The next time you saw him, he was dead, laid out in an open coffin at some out-of-the-way funeral parlor. A dim place, it was, and quiet except for the carpet's asper underfoot. In death, his face was snow again, and he might've been back in Louisville, with those silver slippers and golden horns. And who knows? He might've had a card for once. He might've been inside.

T. S. Eliot, 1888-1965

THE VERDICT

this birth was
Hard and bitter agony for us, like Death
—T.S. Eliot

A life sentence of seventy-seven years, on condition that he spend it as if condemned instead to death: die daily, die all the way, die of the horror outside the skin, the deadly disarray, the I-disease, and die of the horror within it, the mal for another time. He'd've given up being to have been in some myth, the distant kinsman of a god, the custodian of some minor power, sung of rarely and then but in Greek; or he'd've settled for an odd something in the Concordance, a name with a single mention, a bystander, say, a beholder; or, these denied, he'd've squired in this or that Crusade, a braider of manes, a cupbearer, an epicene, even, if such would've made Jerusalem fall; or, because Paradise might've brushed his rags, he'd've been a beggar at the Arno wall. But he drew a bad time for living and a worse one to die.

John Dos Passos, 1896-1970

WORKINGMEN
AND PEOPLE LIKE THAT

I'm not joining anybody.   —John Dos Passos

How could I have strayed so far? By what road of the mind did I wind away? I was one with them once, or, what comes to the same, I warmed at their fire, their aim was mine, their spring I drank from, and the drink it welled was wine. There was a mender of shoes in my pedigree, but he was a long way back in the line, that Portugee, and nearly forgotten by the time I came. For me, it was the Grand Tour, the select *pension*, a tongue of many lingoes, ripeness young, ease, elevation, as someone would say from a cell one day.

But something drew me, people like that, and I flew their signs, walked their files in the shine and rain. I spoke from heights down, crates, cars, flights of steps, I wrote in spates for causes that weren't mine. I misdemeaned in stricken jurisdictions, courted fines and the odium of my kind, journeyed to shrines in other countries, bones in foreign walls, I sought to find the Garden that was gone, the place of no machines. People like that—I broke their bread, I brought back their dead in war, and for the two in Boston (one a shoemaker!), I'd've died, I think, myself.

165

How, then, did I end up here, so lost to the spring, so cold to the fire? I tried to teach them what you taught me (Pio, o Pio Baroja, see o see where I've gone!)—that each man is an *I*, a unity, a life to be lived from inside outward, resisting always, merging never. Beware of systems, I told them, distrust the deeds that're done by crowds, act against thy circumstance, fulfill thyself with being—*be*, I said, and you will bloom, and so will the world and perfume all space. If that was true, my Pio, Pio, how did I reach this place, where I sit among the spoilers, the owners of machines?

I dwell on shoemakers, the one in my blood and the one in that cell near Bunker Hill. I think of workingmen, of Pio Baroja, people like that, and I wonder how they regard me, if ever I cross their mind. What do they say, or do they say nothing, do they merely flick at flies, smile in private, spit? Tell me, Pio, did I betray them with my learning, my well-read eyes, did I lead them down the garden-path but not to any Eden?

How did I get here, in the wilderness where I am?

William Faulkner, 1897-1962

LISTEN TO THE GHOSTS

Then the war came and made the ladies into ghosts. So what else can we do, being gentlemen, but listen to them being ghosts? —William Faulkner

They saunter the town, those lady ghosts, some under the awnings and some, a few, in the sun, they rest in the Square, dappled shades, and there, bowered by the heaven trees, they drowse with old men and their shadows, dogs. And they finger wares, the bygone ladies, filter through the stares of niggers, cut the trash and rednecks cold, and they pass the stone soldier on the monument and the stone pledge on the base—*The sons of veterans unite in this justification of their fathers faith*—and they nod, the ghostly ladies, and go their ghastly way. And as they stroll and stray, they read the signs, the lettered lines of brick—*The Golden Rule*, these say, and *Up Stairs*, and *Patton-Courtney*—and they drift, the spectral ladies, drift the spectral smoke, they cling to the coon-cut lawns, festoon the pine and oak, vine the pillars of the porticoes. And still they traipse, twirling parasols, and now where their path goes, paint peels, and yards are strewn with slain machines, stripped corpses, they seem to be, shoeless, diminished, faded by the rain, and from the crooked doorways, burlap children peer. And then no paint at all do the weightless ladies see, only bare and broken houses blind with paper panes, and there the trees are snags, and the ground is strewn with parts of nothing, pieces that never fit, and beyond all these, niggers blight the cotton fields, a black-and-white disease. And then on to St. Peter's, where they wander, wind, among the mounds and tombs, and there the heat makes the gravestones wave, and a shimmer shakes the air, and they pause, the disembodied ladies, among the disembodied bones, and spelling the name of the beak-nosed man, they speak and say *The sons of veterans* and *their fathers faith*, and six feet down and listening, he hears, he hears the ladies being ghosts.

If you stay there long enough, being gentlemen, you become a part of it.

Hart Crane, 1899-1932

VOYAGES, VII

hold—

Atlantis, —hold thy floating singer late!

—Hart Crane

They put the ship about and crisscrossed the wake, but all they found was what they'd tossed him, a life-buoy broaching a block-letter name: S.S. *Orizaba*. All morning, she'd been steaming north in the Straits of Florida, her speed the better for the four-knot Stream, the running road that ran her way. On the wind, her smoke went too, towing her, and birds, their screaming thinned, and in the noonday sun, like small change strewn, schools of mullet broke and flashed. It was then, they say, that he'd come on deck, gone to the taffrail, and jumped into the champagne scum simmering from the stern. They made the turn and searched for an hour, they gave him two bells of their time.

Did he go in slow motion down to where some cankered anchor lay, some molluscan ewer, a pair of old-world earrings in newer-world lees? Or did he straightway join the past, was he shredded then and there, a great barbless bait, ingested even to the rags he wore, to his own and his buttons' bone, his cut-glass brain, and the deposits of time accrued in his blood? Or did he never, as he'd prayed, submerge at all?

They beat up their wake, seeking him where they'd been before, but why, in that hour, could he not have been borne four knots onward by the Stream? Why must he have sunk, shunned, voided, spewn, why could he not have ridden the flume psalming the Cold Wall and the warm weed, the *Monitor* as he cruised above it, the bluefins in between? Hold! he'd cried, whereat why would the Stream not stay him from the sea's black fractures while he phrased for squids, arrow-worms, anemones, eels, lilies growing in submarine groves, for pelagic snails and tidal reeds? Why would he not spin forever on the gyre, and why, once each round, would he not play upon a mile-wide lyre strung across a harbor sky?

Thomas Wolfe, 1900-1938

A FEAST
NOT MADE FOR LAUGHTER

He was hungry all the time.   —Thomas Wolfe

He was a lifelong appetite, a world-wide mouth ringent for the whole wide world—and all that poured therefrom, all such and more did he raven, the fruits and flowers, the cates and sweet gums, the heaps of wheat, the wine. It was a craze, that need of his to feed, to fill his animal: prey, the planet might've been, and he seemed to take it in his teeth and tear it on the run. The stone and the stream, he devoured, the peak and the subterrane, named places and the spaces in between, distance, time, death, and the very earth he lived on, all of it he ate, and still his ring-tailed roarer raged, until, having greeded down his host, he began to consume himself. He died of that consumption—tb of the brain, they called it, but what killed him was his beast, with that lupine feast in fear of famine.

Before he went, though, there was a great drench, not forty days of high water, but well-nigh forty years of words, and toward the end, as darkness fell, Deluge. It was as if, having crammed all he could, he meant to vent it back, and in his latter days, language simply swithined from him, spewed from his mouth, gushed from his arm, sprang with his sweat and sperm. Acre-feet of utterance, there were, and its level rose, rose, until that lesion in his lung let go and those tubercles flowed in a flood of their own to his brain.

That creature of his was there when the brain stopped, it was in at the kill, and for all one knows, it's still at work on the skull or on the wig it wore to hide the trepanation, or is it gnawing Tom's clothes now, the somber suit, the shirt, the moldering tie, eating the chill and quiet air—or is it less than quiet there these days, do the words fall yet, from the mind and mouth that've gone, do the words still fall, still rain?

Ernest Hemingway, 1899-1961

THE BLOOD-LETTER

You'd remember, on the day he died, how surprised you were at his age. Only a little over sixty, he'd be, a low number for all that noise and motion, all those bottles and executions, for so many words on paper and spoken words, a low number for all his goings-up and comings-down, his wrecks and wars and afternoons in the *sol y sombra*. Near the end, he'd look older than he was, and his gait would be older, and his voice, and he'd *read* older, write as if sixty were already sixty years behind him. His friends would learn what his ex-friends knew, that he had a mean streak in him: he'd get between you and a bear, but when the bear was taken care of, as like as not he'd turn on you. You'd learn to keep mum when he ran himself up and others down, when he planned one of those games of his, those campaigns to make something living become something dead. You'd take no trips with him, or none but the first—he'd run the show, he'd choose the roads and rooms and tell you how your days would go. You'd steer clear of his dromes and cirques, his armorers, and the sporting bars where he held soirées. That mean streak, it would always transpire through his much-man grace, and it'd be wise, you'd find, to let him blow about a mind and eyes that never lied and such exactitudes as *lovely*. You'd wonder at such a world, where all that mattered was how you took the slug, the gaff, the sword, the horn. You'd all be fair game there, for him, for death: if you were brave and stood ill luck well, he'd slap your back and score you high; if not, he wouldn't even crap on your grave. He'd be big, fast, tough, and dumb, like America, and he'd last till his dying day—and before he went, he'd take his limit of unicorns, German browns, and you.

Nathanael West, 1903-1940

MISS LONELYHEARTS
IN THE ADIRONDACKS

The road went through a wild-looking stretch of woods and
they saw some red squirrels and a partridge. . . .
— Nathanael West

He'd just written the sentence, you supposed, or just revised
it, and he was reading it aloud, trying the leanness of the prose,
the sound, the rhythm, and through a partition of two thin coats
of papered plaster, you could hear him phrase in the next-door
room. You could almost see the sheet he read from, ascrawl with
that lurching hand of his, half script, half printing, and
downhill all, the same letters formed in different ways, with
gaunt caps and lank descenders, ungainly, spasmic—like him,
it was. He seemed ill-assembled, you thought, a morph made of
spare parts and odd sizes, each with a will of its own, and he had
a plural way of going, as if he contained a brawl. You heard a
match strike, and you heard it flare, and you called up his
cupped and quavering hands, and you saw smoke climb his face
and gray his hair, and then he read aloud his words for a scene
that might've been mounted on his windowpane.

> *. . . Two deer and a fawn came down to the water on the*
> *opposite side of the pond. . . .*

In his grasp, a pencil became a sixth finger hostile to the other
five, a stiff and sullen balking thing—held by him, all objects
were grim and intervenient, and he was ever at odds with a
cigarette, a hat, a shotgun, a knife and fork, a steering-wheel.
There were many hazards in his world, many enemies, and on a
day still nine years off, one such would prove ineluctable, and
he'd die in a debacle of metal far from where he was now, in a
cabin on Viele Pond, six miles west of Warrensburg on the way
to Stony Creek.

> *. . . It was very sad under the trees . . . in the deep shade there*
> *was nothing but death—rotten leaves, gray and white*
> *fungi. . . .*

171

Death would wait nine years for him to reach a certain road-crossing three thousand miles away, and when he got there, it would break into his brain and expunge its pictures of a summer in the woods. There'd be no screen showing him a spring-fed pond in a cattail ring, there'd be no wind, no cowlicks on the water, no reeds that seemed to run: where such memories had been, there'd be extravasated blood, spalls of bone, a great and pulsing brilliance. His heart would fibrillate for one more hour, and he'd die, and thereafter it would lie with you to make that summer live.

> *. . . The water was so cold that they could only stay in for a short time. . . .*

Sitting there at your window, staring at the same view he had from his, you couldn't know that each of those summer days should've been set down as it went—each day, with all that was said and done. You couldn't know that he'd be gone so soon, giving you custody of that part of his life, you couldn't know that they might matter, his sayings and doings, his ways, his likes, the holes you found in his coat and the ones he found in yours—there'd be time to remember, you thought, and what you forgot you could always get from him. There were jots in the journal of your mind, notes of the bass you took from the Hudson, the paper and living targets you fired at, the wood-stove meals, the smoke sucked into the coal-oil lamps, the talk (what did you say to him, for God's sake!, and what did he say to you?), the do-nothing afternoons, the scrivening sessions on opposite sides of a wall. You'd remember it all.

> *. . . The new green leaves hung straight down and shone in the hot sun like an army of little metal shields. . . .*

Of that summer, buried under forty-five years, the only hard tokens are a spread of snapshots foxed now with age. In them, two figures stand, sit, lounge, two faces are fixed (on what? on whom?), hands hold sticks, a magazine, cigarettes, and an old car can be seen, and a porch, a doorway, a basin near a bench, and there are brown trees, sepia grass, and a tan sky. You have only to wait, you fancy, and you'll hear sound and witness motion: the cigarettes you hold will burn to the end, pages will be read and turned, the day will wear, and to something that one of you has said, the other will make a reply—you need only wait.

But it won't do! it won't do! There'd be no change, though you looked and listened forever. There'd be the same two likenesses of that single moment, stock-still and silent, and they'd tell only what they told before, one particular time, like a stopped clock.

> *. . . Somewhere in the woods a thrush was singing. Its sound was like that of a flute choked with saliva.*

Countee Cullen, 1903-1946

HIGH SCHOOL ON 59th ST.

Yet do I marvel at this curious thing:
To make a poet black, and bid him sing!
— Countee Cullen

In your time at De Witt, there were two blacks, or two you knew of, among a thousand whites: for all those rooms and halls and flights of stairs, all those books, boards, and windowed walls, you were aware of only two. You never wondered, meaning you never cared, about the black multitude that stared at the doors from Harlem, half the town away. Through some seepage or intromission, you sensed their presence, but they were still somewhere else, present *there*, and it didn't pertain to you that but two of their number found the way to San Juan Hill.

About one of them, no more than a particular remains in your mind, a single point, a brass tack, less than his name and only this: he came to class one day with a pistol. Memory of him begins and ends there, on the selfsame downright fact: the pistol. The ins and outs, if ever they were known to you, are gone now, why the gun was carried and why and where drawn,

173

whether it was loaded and, if so, whether it would shoot, gone such things, along with how the news was spread (by a rumor running the corridors? by a stir that sped the stairs?), and gone as well the punishment—death, was it, or did they let the nigger go?

You never said the word, but in your head, you never used another. There in your sequestered self, it was always nigger, soundless since there was no ear. All the same, the Clinton pair seemed to hear the slur you cast in secret—a current, it must've caused, and when they entered your galvanized sphere, you could almost see them stiffen. They knew, they knew: one of the two brought a pistol to school.

The other tried to sing, to soar on lyrics till the pull of g was nil, and he lost the need for feet. Up there, he'd find no white realms where his image was refused by your eye, where no passion was, no dispassion, no hand for and none against him, no place for him to be or not to be. He'd find no color in space but his own. Up there, he'd fly!

His songs were heavier than air, a mourning more than music, and they never set him free, never flew him. *To make a poet black, and bid him sing!* he said—but was it black that weighed him down, or was black made heavy because of such as you?

John Steinbeck, 1902-1968

THE *EAST OF EDEN* LETTERS

There seem to be dead places in a man. —John Steinbeck

They were written on the left-hand pages of a notebook, face to face with the manuscript—on the verso, they were, the even-numbered side of each sheet. All through a nine-month span, he began each day with a message, posted, so to say, but undelivered, a dead letter, really, and only then, when he'd set

174

down an opinion or two, noted the view from his window, stated his state of mind, only then did he take up a pencil, always a round one, and turn to the blank at the right, a white void waiting to be filled with *work*. *Work* is what he called his daily truck with words.

A strange and mystic business, writing.

They were a kind of priming of his mind, those letters, a way to make its still water run, overbrim its pools. He was fifty at the time, give or take a year, and nothing freely flowed any more, nothing poured down the mountains and tumbled toward the sea. And so he fed in reports on sleep, a lot, a little, or none at all, on the condition of his eyes and teeth (*last week two inlays fell out*), on a broken chair he'd mended, on a haircut he meant to get, and he spent sentences on pencils, complained of their shape, the way they wore, their price.

It is a strange thing, a story.

On this dun drift, an occasional glint, a fear he'd had, a bell less heard than apprehended, a telling of the time. But it slowly went, that flash, slowly it was borne away by the rill that was left of his river, a trickle of numbers, calculations, predictions, a slow-motion of entries about his children, wives, household intermissions, about the cage he'd made for his nightingale and the story he was writing on the opposite page.

There are strange things in people.

The book across the way, the one beyond the fold, it'd be his best, he told himself, it summed all the rest of his books (*work* was the word he used), it was about his tribe, the forces that came together in him, the courses they took in his blood and brain, it was about the life he had to live with, his one and only road. But seated there at his sloping desk, defended by trays of pointed pencils (Mongol, Calculator, Blackwing), secure among his little improvements and inventions, encased in words (a thousand more each day!)—still, with his doubts and disclaimers of doubt, he seemed to wonder about the fifteen years just gone and the fifteen yet to come.

What strange aches we get, a kind of sick weariness.

What got into a man, he may have thought, or what that was in went out? What power was lost with time, what did it cost to age? Had he used himself up, or had some of him, unused, run away? Strange, strange, he may have mused, strange and terrible his dreams, and this now went through his mind, that if a man knew what his life would be, he'd refuse to live it, and he wrote the thought down, and he wrote these things too, that he'd made a tool-rack, that pencils were a great expense, that people rarely sang for joy.

Now, once to the toilet and I will go to work.

Once to the toilet, he wrote on a left-hand page.

Lionel Trilling, 1905-1975

"MAXIM HAS BROKEN"

"Broken?" said Arthur. "What do you mean, broken?"
—Lionel Trilling

Broken, Laskell had said, as if Maxim had been something allowed to drop, a platter, a vase, a figurine, and shatter on the floor. *Maxim has broken* —and there he was, fractions of glass or china, fingers, toes, a nose, an ear, behold what once was Gifford Maxim, a disjunct union. Laskell had spoken scholastic cant, of course, and by *broken* he'd meant a predicate too, for the action pent in the verb, but Arthur was dense, a pipe-sucking gent, hence *Broken? What do you mean broken?* And Laskell, lately in love with the dimsome rose of death (scarlet fever? scarlet Marx?), Laskell had said *Broken with the Communist Party*. It lay there, Maxim's deed, like someone dear dying. Not Giff! not Giff!—ah, but Giff it was, Giff in shivareens.

Thinkers, they thought they were, but they couldn't believe that he'd stopped believing. What shocked, what shook them so was this: that a belief could end. To them, who'd never begun, who'd believed only in Giff's belief, it was simply voltaic that Giff was done with belief, that thenceforward they must find

176

another fire or freeze, another faith or flounder, horses in the mire. They were betrayed by Giff's betrayal, as if somehow, in the sale of himself, he'd conveyed them too.

But being thinkers, reasonable men, tame, they were able to sit at the same board, able to bread-and-wine it with Max imMarxed, Giff the renegade. And he made the most of it, their still-dear near-dead Judas: being allowed to explain, he explained his God away. He did not cast his silver down nor die on the field of blood: he lived to yield up others for the silver of some coming day.

Leonard Ehrlich, 1905-

GOD'S ANGRY MAN

They were hunting John Brown as they hunted a wolf. They wanted him dead or living, better dead.
　　　　　　　　　　　　　　　—Leonard Ehrlich

It took him four years to write the book and the four ahead to prepare it, or twice four, or, who can say now?, it may have taken all his life. Something may have been there when he was born, in or on the air, a name spoken, a sigh, a sound as of a dry stick broken, and if so, may it not have early found the slight and blackhaired city Jew—where?, was it in the Bronx that he first came to light, in Harlem that he played, or Brighton Beach? and by whom was the critical sonant made, someone of the breed, friend, teacher, stranger passed in the street?

What drew the dark and delicate Jew to Brown is now no longer remembered. He was drawn, that much he knew, there was some (or a seeming) attraction, and it tranced the man, enraptured him—a kind of capillarity, there may have been between the two, the Jew and Brown, and the two became one, and the one Messianic. The writing was darksome, doomful, a four-hundred-page continuation of the attainder on the Wall.

177

They were lit, where lit at all, by lavender lightnings, and there was murder under that overcast, and lunacy, and a sense of flow toward an endless fall.

He was born in Brown. He burned in Brown's fire, said the same isaian words, shed with Brown the blood of slavers. He too conceived that fond-blinded insurrection (pikes for arms!), stormed the Ferry arsenal, and, with the same high-minded handful, failed. Four hundred pages, his lifeline ran, and there'd be more such books, he proclaimed, a series similar in aim, depicting other scourges in the making, other selves in other Browns.

But thereafter, sad to say, more pages never came: he'd spent them all on Brown. When the trap was sprung—and he, in writing, sprang it—he fell too (a sound as of a dry stick broken), dangled for thirty-seven minutes, and in the strangled martyr, in John Brown's body, died.

John O'Hara, 1905-1970

THE END OF LANTENENGO ST.

If you are an author, and not just a writer, you keep learning
all the time.   —John O'Hara

He was after the badges, he wrote somewhere. He was well on the way then, and he had all the rest, the lands in fee and the chattels real, he had the movables, bespoke and otherwise, and knowing that his span was spinning out, he yearned for bays to be wound in his hair, he wanted the honors he thought he'd earned, the cap-and-gowned doctorates, the prizes, the scholarly mentions in notes and text—badges, he called such things, and he hankered for them.

Words flooded from his arm. He had merely to point at blank paper, it seemed, and the spate would start, the freshet flow. Scenes would spread and stories run—a marvel, that

178

fictive font of his, it would dry up never, that ever-fluent stream. But it was the same fluid always, and you came to think that he had only one tale to tell, one view of the same few people, that there was only one place he knew of, one town, one street, even, and it stiff with spitting images.

They were ringers for each other, that numerous cast: they could've swapped clothes and speech, homes, mates, lovers, lives, and when one of them went, his dent would be filled by one still here. Permutation was their essence: each would've yielded spare parts for all. They were quiet, those snots in his muster of bastards, their manners were assault without battery, their couplings were cool confusions of pubic hair, rather thoughtful, really, and very nearly dry, and, day in and day out, they made the same unsignal round.

You keep learning all the time, he said, but his last book was his first, and what followed was simply more—the same old listless fornications, the same snake-cold venom, the same craze for the proper name (it was *Seckel* pear, you were told). An elevation of his life would've shown no heights, no depressions—it would've been a straight line with a slight slope downward. A very gradual grade, it'd have, like that street he imagined and found so real. Those he wrote of still live there: he never moved them out, never wanted them out, and they never let him in.

Richard Wright, 1908-1960

CRÈCHE 4596, PÈRE LACHAISE

How calm I've felt in Paris!   —Richard Wright

Strange, to wind up here, a pound or two of ash, the residue of a black man burned dead for once instead of alive, strange, for one of his beginning, to be turned at the end to mineral trifles, a handful to fill a Belleville urn. He wasn't supposed to die in bed, not unless he'd bled there first, stained its stains from

179

the stub of his cock and the veins of missing balls. Strange, his wearing in this place, granules crumbling to dust, dust becoming finer dust and one day nothing an ocean away from home.

But then his story was all of it strange, one of his own plots, it might've been, a lifelong night of fear and murder, and sheer as a shadow, he seemed to flounder through it as from something dreamed, in flight (was it flight?) from something black to something white. Is that what it was, that nocturne, flight?, that dim and drawn-out wend from Natchez to the fire? *I have to remind myself that I'm a Negro*, he said. *There are whole days when I forget it*—but if so, it came back to him: he never did shuck his skin, he was still black when he died, black outside and black within. The cause of death was that calm he felt in Paris: it took fifteen years to kill him.

James Agee, 1909-1955

DEATH IN A HACK

Let us now praise . . .   —James Agee

There's no knowing now at what corner he hailed the cab, along Fifth, it may have been, in front of the Cathedral or at some crosstown curb, but it doesn't matter any more, and maybe it never did: he was on the way to his doctor, and he didn't care to walk. Standing there, wherever it was, he may have felt imbalanced, as from a need of more blood in his brain, and he may have leaned against a lamppost for a moment, barely experiencing the cool cast iron, the dark brown paint, and it may have been those faint responses that disinclined him, made the distance to his doctor seem too long, as if he'd worn the wrong kind of shoes. Which ones had he put on that morning?, he may have wondered as he climbed into the cab.

As it turned out, it wouldn't've made any difference if he'd walked. It was a day in May, mild, no doubt, and clear, with a sense of something blooming not too far away, and he might've leisured up the Avenue, past the windows and their wares, their leather, silk, and silver, and had he so desired, he might've smoked as he went, smoked twice, once in the plate glass and once in the open air, and he might've watched girls approach and pass, heard parts of speech, pigeons in the dentils, feet chafing the pavement, the absonant tongues of horns. Who can say now? Might he not have reached the Park?

Instead, though, he rode, eyed the crowds from the inside out, and at some unnumbered street he died, there on that semi-public seat, that place he'd hired for a mile or two, a last breath left him, as it would've done at death in the open air. What thoughts did he have on that foreshortened ride, what words that he'd written reran themselves in his mind, what words he'd meant to write, what time ill-spent, and, if he sensed the end, what time well—? Did he think that something of his, of him, would remain, be read, be heard, retain the power to stir, as he'd been stirred in the creation? Was he reading when he came to the Hour, a paper, the posted list of tariffs, the driver's name, was he scanning the driver's picture, wondering whether the man at the wheel was the same? Or did he feel a fear begin to grow of sockets instead of eyes, did he know that if the head should ever turn. . . . ?

Conrad Aiken, 1889-1973

AT THE GRAVE OF MALCOLM LOWRY

Good night, disgrace.   —Conrad Aiken

In a stand of field-flowers, his low and grassgrown stone, already out of true and at home here in this deadyard, how soon a part of this hummocked world.

Good night, disgrace, I said
when I saw him last, but not in anger, how could I have spoken
to him in anger?, yet I did say it,
　　disgrace, I said,
and others heard and may have thought I meant the sidewalk
meaning of the word, grace gone, a loss of grace,
　　which God forbid,
because I did not hate the damn, the ever-dramming boy. No,
the disgrace was in the glass tit he sucked at, downing swill to
kill his Demon, the disgrace was in the gin he yearned for
turned to vomit, drowning in his own spew, a juniper suicide.
　　Under this camber
of unmown grass and self-sown flowers, the dead drunk lies,
autopsied by coroners and coronary ants, here, all ligatures lost,
the loose ends of friend, son, learner, here at Ripe in Sussex,
here at my feet the brained skull, the sedimented blood, the
hollow where the heart once beat, the sum all come apart, here
in this holy ground the liar, the braggart, the inventor of
myths, dabbler in the arcane, cribber, spiller of seed—but even
so still a *cher élève*, a rare dead son, a dear and bathless seeker of
symbols and correspondences, here underfoot, near enough to
touch.
　　Good night, disgrace, I said,
meaning hands that shook too much for shaving, to let him tie a
tie or light a cigarette, meaning the way he pissed his bed
bemused, the stories true and tall he told, the fall he took in a pit
of shit,
　　good night, disgrace, I said,
meaning his endless bender (or endless till he died and ended),
meaning lost or mislaid things, people, pages, shoes, and time,
meaning disturbances of the peace and mind, meaning arrests
and recoveries, meaning changes of place for the sake of
motion, quests without a quarry, meaning one book to show for
a throwaway life.
　　Disgrace, I said,
but I did not hate you, homeless son, pilgrim on the road that
misses Rome, I did not hate you, swimmer in the sea that has no
shore, I did not hate you, writer of one book worth a score of
mine.

Good night, disgrace, I said,
but I did not hate you.

John Berryman, 1914-1972

THE MISSISSIPPI:
AT THE HEAD OF NAVIGATION

stricken Henry with his sisters & brothers
suddenly gone pauses to wonder why he
alone breasts the wronging tide   —John Berryman

Henry writes a note (to whom?), saying *I'm a nuisance*, and leaving it on a bill-spike or cocked against a clock (whatever the hour, for Henry the time of day is night), he walks across the campus toward the bridge. From the abutment, he can hear the Falls of St. Anthony, and he gazes at a river that one may run from the Gulf to here, twenty-five hundred browngreen miles up the ileum of America, or run from here to there, down those greenbrown sigmoid miles, but Henry knows this, that whichever way he goes, with or against the wronging tide, he will ride the sordure of his own his native land, the slough, the offscum, the national exosmotic slime. He knows, does Henry, the enormities, the okra of wrongs that thickens this stream, this gumbo of guilt, he knows, our Henry, our stricken Henry, and tiring (we must suppose) of breasting the tide alone, he climbs the railing of the bridge (alas!), looks about in a last slow pass, and leaps a hundred feet to death below—not in the river, though, but on its rim of rocks. A suicide, they call the act (*one more suicide?*), but when Tambo speaks, or Bones, the verdict is murder, and the killer's name is known.

    In Henry's pockets, a pair of glasses and a blank check are found, nothing more.

> In the grand national open drain,
> America flows, a riverain crumble,
> A churn of skim and scour wherein
> Clavicles tumble and sawyers turn,

The scale of snakes and flakes of shale,
A shingle (slaver? packet? privateer?)
Launched by a boy on the Cumberland,
And feathers, and wheels of oil,
All these with the slow stream mingle,
And Lovejoy's type is filled with silt,
Salt of tears Abe spilled for Ann, sand,
Ojibway nails and teeth and hair,
And a piece of the True Cross sails
With a fleet of similar splinters,
And swollen dogs roll, and niggers—
All this, the Mississippi. . . .

*Ah sinful nation . . . The cormorant and the bittern shall possess
it.*

This first edition was designed by Marcia Burtt in Santa Barbara, California. Display type by Foster & Horton; Caslon Old Face body type by Charlene McAdams; calligraphy by Emily Paine; camera work by Santa Barbara Photoengravers; printed and bound by R.R. Donnelley & Sons in Crawfordsville, Indiana.

Author's photo by Wayne McCall.